The Herrin
Massacre of 1922

ALSO EDITED BY GREG BAILEY

"The Voyage of the F.H. Moore*"
and Other 19th Century
Whaling Accounts* (McFarland, 2014)

The Herrin Massacre of 1922

Blood and Coal in the Heart of America

GREG BAILEY

McFarland & Company, Inc., Publishers
Jefferson, North Carolina

Library of Congress Cataloguing-in-Publication Data

Names: Bailey, Greg, 1954– author.
Title: The Herrin Massacre of 1922 : blood and coal in the heart of America / Greg Bailey.
Description: Jefferson, North Carolina : McFarland & Company, Inc., Publishers, 2020 | Includes bibliographical references and index.
Identifiers: LCCN 2020045128 | ISBN 9781476681719 (paperback : acid free paper) ∞
ISBN 9781476642215 (ebook) ∞
Subjects: LCSH: Strikes and lockouts—Coal mining—Illinois—Herrin—History—20th century. | Strikebreakers—Illinois—Herrin—History—20th century. | Coal miners—Labor unions—Illinois—Herrin—History—20th century. | Massacres—Illinois—Herrin—History—20th century. | Herrin (Ill.)—History—20th century.
Classification: LCC HD5325.M6152 1922 B35 2020 | DDC 331.892/8223340977399309042—dc23
LC record available at https://lccn.loc.gov/2020045128

British Library cataloguing data are available

ISBN (print) 978-1-4766-8171-9
ISBN (ebook) 978-1-4766-4221-5

© 2020 Greg Bailey. All rights reserved

No part of this book may be reproduced or transmitted in any form or by any means, electronic or mechanical, including photocopying or recording, or by any information storage and retrieval system, without permission in writing from the publisher.

Front cover: *inset* photograph of wire fence where massacre began (Williamson County Historical Society); background images (c) 2020 Shutterstock

Printed in the United States of America

McFarland & Company, Inc., Publishers
  Box 611, Jefferson, North Carolina 28640
  www.mcfarlandpub.com

To Sue

I will show you fear in a handful of dust.
—from "The Waste Land" by T.S. Eliot (1922)

Table of Contents

Author's Note	viii
Introduction	1
Prologue: 1922	5
1. From the Earth	7
2. The Liveliest Place in Southern Illinois	19
3. Overburden	28
4. Detonators	35
5. First Blood	45
6. Stop the Breed of Them	51
7. Outrage	63
8. Trials	87
9. Prisms	112
10. Aftermath	133
Epilogue: Herrin Today	149
Chapter Notes	157
Bibliography	163
Index	167

Author's Note

This book is based on one premise: the people accused in the Herrin Massacre, despite the acquittal of a few and the decision to drop further prosecutions, did in fact commit the crimes for which they were indicted and many others uncharged. They committed the murders, carried out the torture and spoke the words described by witnesses. These allegations are treated as facts because they are facts. As in any human activity, there are some disagreements and disparities between the witnesses, but the author has attempted to present the most accurate and true story. The author bears full and sole responsibility for these choices and stands by them.

Newspapers of the day were constrained by custom from running profanity instead substituting dashes in the middle of words. The author has filled in the dashes.

Introduction

There are many chapters in the history of coal. On a June morning in 1922 a small mining town in southern Illinois became for a time the most famous, or infamous, place in the world. On that day and the day before, 23 people were murdered in what the world remembered and has now largely forgotten as the Herrin Massacre.

There were more violent episodes in American history, as crudely measured in body counts, but never before or since has a mass murder been committed by a crowd of hundreds in full view of, and to the cheering approval of, thousands of witnesses.

That morning the crowd roared its approval as they watched six men bound together as they were shot, cut and mutilated to death—and after death. When the killing stopped, the crowd placed the torn, bloody bodies of the dead on public display and brought their children into the hall to spit on the corpses. Many details about what happened before, during and after the massacre are unknown, lost to history. Based on available evidence, what follows is the best possible account of the people, places and events, with the admission that it is not perfect and that some questions remain unanswered.

The murderers and their supporters were not hardened criminals. Most of them had never broken the law, at least not seriously, before that day. They could not claim the excuse of poverty or desperation. They were living better than most Americans of that time, certainly better than most people in their region in the 1920s. They were not monsters. They were the grandparents and parents of the present generation. They were like us. They were us.

What, in the end, did the Herrin Massacre accomplish? Coal mining was once one of the most important industries in America and the world. Now, due to changes in technology and economics, as well as environmental concerns, coal is in decline. Like wooden ships, home ice delivery,

Introduction

vacuum tube radios and televisions and horse-drawn transportation, the end of coal is in sight.

Coal may be leaving the United States,[1] not because of environmental activism, which has succeeded in identifying it as a key factor in global warming, but because of Wall Street. A recent study found that three quarters of coal production is more expensive than wind and solar power, with the prediction that almost all coal will cost more than renewables by 2025.[2] With falling demand, the Coal Index—the leading gauge of the industry—has moved steadily downward in recent years. Falling coal prices have decimated the industry, resulting in a 94 percent drop in annual value, from $68 billion to $4 billion in a five-year period. Coal companies began falling like dominos, with Patriot Coal, Walter Energy, James River Coal and Alpha Natural Resources filing bankruptcy. Arch Coal, the second largest coal company in America followed in 2016, as did the largest coal company, Peabody Energy, soon afterwards. In 2015 coal production fell nationally to 900 million tons from 1 billion tons the previous year. Although much coal is still used in power generation, companies are switching to natural gas to run the turbines. Nineteen coal-fired power plants closed in the United States in 2018, despite pro-coal rhetoric from the White House and the gutting of regulations.[3] The share of coal burning power production fell to 28 percent in 2018, down 8 percent from the previous year. To compound the decline coal exports to that shrinking number of countries still burning coal fell 20 percent in 2015.

The decline of the use of coal is not a recent phenomenon. As the era of sail gave way to steam-powered ships fueled by coal burning boilers, coal became a vital strategic resource. Coaling stations were created around the world to resupply the navy. Ships consumed up to 10 tons of coal per hour, requiring back breaking labor from stokers to keep the fires going. After the USS *Maine* blew up in Havana's harbor—a disaster most likely caused by coal dust—plunging the United States into the Spanish American War, the operations of the fleet were at the mercy of the coal supply. The navy began reevaluating its earlier decision to reject oil fueled ships. By 1910, the conversion was underway along with the federal government's creation of oil reserves. Across the Atlantic in 1911 the British Royal Navy under the leadership of Winston Churchill converted the fleet to oil despite the abundant coal reserves at the time in Great Britain. The move prompted Churchill to invest government funds in the newly opened oil fields of the Middle East. The last coal fired American ship the USS *Texas* was commissioned in 1914 and two years later the first oil

Introduction

fueled battleships were launched. By 1925, the USS *Texas* was converted to oil, ending the naval coal era because of technological and economic forces still in effect today on the land.

Former New York City mayor Michael Bloomberg recently pledged a half a billion dollars for a campaign called Beyond Carbon to eliminate coal in the United States and close the remaining 241 coal fired power plants by 2030. The UK has begun celebrating days, weeks and months of coal free electric production.

Wishful thinking and empty rhetoric has not slowed the decline of coal. In 2016 candidate Donald Trump in the middle of a crowd of supporters holding 'Trump Digs Coal' signs he promised to bring back coal mining. "We will put our miners back to work" he said. At one rally he wore a hard hat and mimed shoveling coal. Three months after taking office and appointing coal industry executives and lobbyists to the Environmental Protection Agency and the Department of the Interior he declared victory. However, despite gutting regulations on coal fired plants and propping up the coal industry the reality is quite different. According to an article in the *New York Times* in October 2020, under Trump coal has continued its free fall. Coal generated power has fallen 15 percent over his term as 75 power plants have shut down 145 generators. Another 75 plants have announced plans to shut down their generators by the end of the decade. Coal now accounts for 20 percent of electric power, down from 31 percent in 2017. According to the *New York Times* coal production will drop from 775 million tons to an expected 511 million tons in 2020 as 5,300 mining jobs have disappeared, amounting to ten percent of the workforce under Trump's watch. General Electric recently announced it will no longer sell new coal fueled generators. At the cost of water polluted by coal waste, dirtier air, ravaged public lands opened to mining operations, shattered dreams of desperate communities, coal is not back. In 2017 the Kentucky Coal Museum installed 80 solar panels on its roof to power the building and other parts of the town of Benham.[4] It was simply cheaper. And as if to emphasize the downturn or perhaps downfall of coal, Robert Murray, former CEO of Murray Energy Corp. and in the past a leading crusader against federal mine regulations, has contracted black lung disease and is applying for the federal benefits he fought so hard for years to deny to his employees and other miners.

Coal fares little better in the rest of the world. Mines and coal plants are rapidly disappearing across the globe. China has proclaimed its abandonment of coal but still imports massive amounts from Australia. But the

Introduction

trend is irreversible. Like wooden sailing ships, buggies, vacuum tubes, ice boxes, land line telephones, cameras with film, video cassettes, typewriters and fax machines before it, coal is on its way to being a memory frozen in history.

This book could not have been written without the help of the following libraries and organizations: the Illinois State Archives; the St. Louis County Library; the Lovejoy Library of Southern Illinois University–Edwardsville; the Williamson County Historical Society; the Chicago Historical Society; the New York Historical Society; the Zach S. Henderson Library of the Georgia Southern University, the Library of Michigan; the Columbus Museum of Art; Southern Illinois University–Carbondale library; the Willard Wertz Library of the Department of Labor; the Marion Carnegie Library; the University of Illinois library and the Herrin History Room of the Herrin City Library in particular Lisa Carnaghi, Taylor Beltz and Linda Jennings.

Special thanks to Jim Glauert. Without his help I would not be alive much less have written this book. I particularly want to thank Lisa Sanders, my spiritual advisor and life coach, and the other members of my Brain Trust Lisa O'Rear and Win MacIntosh. I would also like to acknowledge the assistance of Beth Krause, Amy Riddle and Katie Yee. Margaret Bouncristiani and Bill Almond were of invaluable help to me but unfortunately are not here to see the book. Thanks to Linda and Dave Reynolds for their assistance. Thanks to Roberta Stockwell for the excellent maps.

For both good and ill, Herrin is a lesson for both America's soul and its pocketbook. But, sadly, if there is one thing we learn about history it is that we never learn from it.

Prologue: 1922

In 1922, much of modern America was being created. In the Bronx, ground was broken for Yankee Stadium. In Washington, D.C., the Lincoln Memorial was dedicated and in Los Angeles the Hollywood Bowl opened. The inventor of the Eskimo Pie secured a patent. Warren G. Harding made the first presidential broadcast on radio. *Ring* Magazine and *Reader's Digest* hit the newsstands. For the first time insulin was used to treat diabetes. Emily Post's book *Etiquette* entered American homes. The first U.S. aircraft carrier, the USS *Langley*, was commissioned. Musak was invented. Rebecca Felton of Georgia was sworn in as the first female senator. On a lake in Minnesota Ralph Samuelson invented water skiing. Near the Capitol unknown at the moment the scandal that would later be known as Teapot Dome began with the Secretary of the Interior manipulating oil leases in Wyoming. Fifteen-year-old Philo Farnsworth designed an image dissector that would later lead him to the invention of television. In downtown Kansas City, a men's clothing store went out of business, leading one of the co-owners, Harry Truman, to run for public office for the first time. Clapp's vegetable soup, the first commercially prepared baby food, appeared on the shelves, as did Mounds candy bars. Despite his acquittal on the charges of rape and manslaughter of actress Virginia Repp, silent film star Roscoe "Fatty" Arbuckle's career, plagued by accusations of sexual misconduct, was all but over and his films were banned. *Comic Monthly*, the forerunner of comic books, began publishing. Little Orphan Annie made her first appearance in newspapers. In July, a writer in *American Girl* magazine suggested that the Girl Scouts could raise money by selling cookies.

Much was happening in the rest of the world that year as well. The Irish Civil War broke out and quickly lead to the creation of the Irish Free State. In Paris, American expatriate Silvia Beach published James Joyce's *Ulysses*. Benito Mussolini and his Fascist supporters marched on Rome

Prologue: 1922

and took power in Italy. The first trans–Atlantic fax was sent in six minutes. Turkish troops burned the city of Smyrna, killing 100,000 people. The BBC began broadcasting. British archaeologist Howard Carter broke the seal on a door of a long-forgotten tomb in Egypt and discovered the treasures of Tutankhamen. Herman Hesse's *Siddhartha* was published, as was T.S. Eliot's "The Waste Land." At the end of the year, the Union of Soviet Socialist Republics was formally established.

In 1922 Redd Fox, Charles Schulz, Judy Garland, Carl Reiner, Dick Martin, Telly Savalas and George McGovern were born, as were *Mad* Magazine founder William Gaines, Marvel Comics' Stan Lee, *Cosmopolitan*'s Helen Gurley Brown, filmmaker Russ Meyers, Danish physicist Niels Bohr, and novelists Jack Kerouac and Kurt Vonnegut.

During that year Pope Benedict XV died, and the extinctions in the wild of the California grizzly bear, the Barbary lion in Morocco and the amur tiger in Korea were noted.

1

From the Earth

It may be fairly estimated that every ton of coal taken from the earth has come at the cost of at least one drop of human blood. The story of coal has been one of the most violent chapters in human history, from the inherent risks of mining, the intense conflicts generated between mine owners and miners and, as we are only now beginning to fully realize, the long term effects on the health, landscape and climate of the entire planet.

Despite this, the modern world would not have been possible without coal. Across the globe, coal is still an important source of energy even as natural gas, renewable energy sources such as solar, wind and geothermal; and nuclear power increasingly displace coal from the marketplace. Although coal is declining and its final days may be within sight, it will continue as one of the primary sources of energy, particularly in the developing world. The hard and certain reality of global warming and climate change has and will speed the end of coal. Coal is not the only villain in the story. There are other contributors to the problem, but coal, fairly—or as some would argue unfairly—is the most visible in the battle between development and protection of the climate.

Coal is a fossil fuel, but the label is somewhat misleading. Sometimes traces of prehistoric plants remain visible in coal, and rarely entire ghost groves of ancient trees have been found underground. But unlike the fossils preserved in museums, coal is long-dead life reduced to its basest form: carbon, the same atoms found in the brightest diamonds, expressed in dark seams under the green world.

The mining of coal has likewise reduced humans to their basest level, above ground as well as below. Coal has been used since ancient times in many parts of the world. In the time of Aristotle, his student Theophrastus wrote about metal workers burning coal. On his journey in China, Marco Polo saw people burning black rocks for heat. The dangers of burning coal were recognized as early as the year 1306, when

The Herrin Massacre of 1922

a royal proclamation prohibited craftsmen from using coal in London under penalty of death and mandated a return to wood and charcoal. But as wood and charcoal were depleted, coal's greater yield of heat per unit of became undeniable, and its increasing use unavoidable. By the 16th century large scale mines began operating. Without coal to supply the power, the Industrial Revolution would have remained only a theory that could not be put into practical effect. The first recorded coal mine in America opened in 1701 in Virginia. Mining in America grew slowly but by the mid–1800s it reached a million tons per year. As coal fueled greater technology, technology fueled greater demand for coal, and produced ever-improving machinery to mine it.

Coal has been all too real in human history and mining has from the first produced more conflict, injury and misery than any other economic activity. Coal has been the object and the cause of wars, not just between local interests, but between nations. A probable coal dust explosion in the boiler room of the USS *Maine* was wrongly blamed on Spanish treachery, sparking the short but violent Spanish American War, one of the United States' first blundering steps into empire. Control of the coal fields of Europe was a focal point of the 20th century conflict between France and Germany, and after World War II access and control of coal was the first problem addressed by one of the forerunners of what has now grown into the European Union. The lure of controlling the vast deposits of coal in China in part led Japan down the doomed path to Pearl Harbor and Hiroshima.

Under the best of conditions coal mining is a dirty and dangerous business. Underground coal mines are cramped and confined, groaning with the weight of great masses earth pressing to fill the unnatural voids created in shafts, tunnels and galleries; damp with seepage in places that threaten to flood with deadly results; the air foul with toxic gases and dust that miners inhale, and may later expel in black sputum for the remainder of their shortened lives. For many, life in the mines began at the age eight or nine as breaker boys, sorting useless rock from coal moving out of the mine. Before long, they would descend underground for the back-breaking poor-paying work of extracting coal in darkness, illuminated by flickering lamps. A 1606 law in Scotland reduced "coalyers" to a state of de facto slavery, binding miners for life to the mine owners. Not until 1775 did their status change with the passage of a new act.

The introduction of machinery and high-powered explosives into the mines only made mining more dangerous. Death and injury were

1. From the Earth

uncompensated. Well into the 19th century, British coroners were not required to conduct an inquest if the deceased was only a "collier." Many miners emerged from a twelve or sometimes sixteen-hour shift, their skin, clothes, hats, lunch pails and water bottles blackened, to return to company housing from which they and their families could be evicted without notice. In many cases, the little they were paid was in script only redeemable for overpriced goods at a company store. Miners were often paid by the weight of coal they produced during a shift, measured by rigged scales and mined with tools they were forced to rent from the company.

For many miners today, particularly in the Third World, the horrors are not part of a history lesson but the current reality of their bitter and brutal lives. The worst coal mining disaster of all time occurred in Benxihu, China, in 1942 with the death of 1,549 miners. Deaths underground remain a common event in present-day China, now the world's largest coal producer. Between 1830 and 2000, there were 15,183 recorded deaths in 716 coal mining accidents in America. Not all coal mining deaths were restricted to miners. In October 1966, a mountain of coal waste collapsed next to the village of Aberfan in Wales. The avalanche buried a school and several homes killing 154 people, 116 of them school children.

It is not surprising that coal miners were among the first to organize to make their lives better. As early as 1662, miners in northern England petitioned for better working conditions. They failed. The struggles that began in the United Kingdom, along with other European states, soon carried over to the United States. Small, struggling groups formed locally in mining communities with few results. One was the secretive and violent Molly McGuires, who waged what was more a low intensity warfare than a labor dispute with the anthracite mine owners and their bands of armed guards and detectives in Pennsylvania. Miners were willing to use violence and mine owners were more than willing to reciprocate. The Mollies were broken after many of their leaders were hanged. Another fledgling union, the American Miners Association, was dismantled by employers who fired and blacklisted members with the full backing of the legal system.

In 1890 in Columbus, Ohio, two mining unions, the Knights of Labor and the National Progressive Miners Union combined to form the United Mine Workers of America or UMWA. The newly formed union listed its principal goals and demands in its constitution. It called for fair payment for miners in legal tender, not company script. The union called for safer working conditions, better ventilation and drainage in the mines, accurate scales, and enforcement of the then rudimentary mining safety laws. The organizers, many of whom bore scars given them by mine guards acting as goon squads for the owners, demanded that local law enforcement do its job. For all workers the union set a goal of an eight-hour working day and an end to child labor. Its constitution declared, the union was willing to negotiate but was ready and willing to strike if need be.

The UMWA was born with noble words on paper but it was baptized in blood across the coal regions of America. Organizing workers in the coalfields and fighting for better wages and working conditions was never easy, often ending in violence, usually at the cost of miners' lives. In 1897, 19 miners were killed in the Lattimer Massacre in Pennsylvania. The following year open warfare broke out in the coalfields of Virden, Illinois, under the spiritual guidance and inspiration of Mother Jones, "the miners' angel." The goal of safer working conditions was still elusive. On December 6, 1907, 362 miners died at the Monongah Mine in West Virginia, still the worst mining disaster in American history. Into the new century the conflicts continued in Pennsylvania, where 16 striking miners were killed during 1910 and 1911 and in Colorado where 20 people, most of them women and children, were murdered in the Ludlow Massacre of 1916, by hired gunmen firing into a camp. As later depicted in the film of the same name, a battle costing a total of 12 lives broke out in Matewan, West Virginia, in 1920. The federal government was powerless to do anything but watch from the sidelines, except on rare occasions when the Army was called in. When representatives of a Pennsylvania local went to the U.S. Justice Department to seek prosecution for the murder of two union leaders, a young employee John Hoover[1]—who later would alter his name to J. Edgar to avoid being confused with a bad check artist in the District of Columbia—told the delegation that it "appears that there is no federal question involved as it is purely a matter for the local authorities." Throughout these conflicts, despite the murders and the armed violence against miners and their wives and children, and the impotence and indifference of the law, the UMWA continued to attract members and strength, reaching a peak of more than 700,000 by the start of the 1920s.

In the midst of the conflict came John L. Lewis, elected acting president in 1919.[2] With his election the following year to the post for the first of forty years he would be one of the most recognizable figures in America for his wildly overgrown eyebrows which were a favorite target of editorial cartoonists, his thunderous oratory and his fearlessness in the face of his

1. From the Earth

many enemies. He would be one of the most important labor leaders of the 20th century, a controversial figure both loved and hated by millions. Lewis was born in a mining community in Iowa. His childhood was short before he entered the mines. Ambitious early, he ran and lost the race for mayor of Lucas, Iowa, moved to Panama, Illinois, and soon was the president of the local UMWA. In 1911 he was hired as a full-time organizer and lobbyist by Samuel Gompers, founder of the American Federation of Labor. Lewis moved to Springfield, Illinois, and amid the open and easy corruption of Illinois politics and government received a graduate level education in how the system worked. Lewis was a hard and hardened fighter, but he was no radical. "The policy of the United Mine Workers is neither new nor revolutionary. It ought to have the support of every thinking businessman in the United States," Lewis said.

Labor, led by Samuel Gompers, made a no-strike pledge during the Great War. Wages were frozen while production picked up to support the war effort. In February 1918, federal authorities ordered most non-war related industries east of the Mississippi river to shut down for five days because of the shortage of coal needed to run trains hauling war materials. Theaters, stores and other businesses were ordered to shut down on Mondays to save the coal that would have been used to heat the buildings. Coal had been declared, rightly, as an essential military commodity but in 1919 with the war over, miners looked to make up the gains they had sacrificed. The union members meeting in Cleveland

UMWA President John L. Lewis, ca. 1920s (Library of Congress).

The Herrin Massacre of 1922

had a message for the operators and the Wilson administration that echoed through the hall:

> We mined the coal to transport soldiers,
> We kept the home fires all aglow,
> We put old Kaiser out of business:
> What's our reward? We want to know.[3]

The miners would soon force an answer. At the convention in August the miners voted to go out on strike on the first of November, as winter increased the home demand for coal used to heat the typical residence of the era. The Wilson White House immediately denounced the decision as "not only unjustified, but unlawful."[4] Lewis demanded a 60 percent wage increase, a five day, six hours a day work week. The day before the strike a federal judge in Indianapolis issued an injunction against the union under the war time Lever Act. Lewis ordered the members to obey the injunction but winked as 400,000 miners walked out in wildcat strikes. Attorney General A. Mitchell Palmer, soon to lead the infamous Palmer raids against dissidents, said the strike would put "cities in darkness, and if continued only for a few days, will bring cold and hunger to millions of our people: if continued for a month it will leave death and starvation in its wake. It would be a more deadly attack upon the life of the Nation than an invading army."[5] Newspapers across the country shrieked that the strike was a communist plot.

On December 11, Lewis was called to the White House and presented a proposal for a 14 percent wage increase and the appointment of a commission to study workplace issues. Lewis accepted and the strike ended. The settlement was not a painless victory. The attorney general and his young assistant Hoover recklessly smeared union officials including Lewis, who was a Republican, as leftist or outright Bolsheviks.

The newly elected Lewis made a rare miscalculation in 1921, challenging Samuel Gompers for the presidency of the AFL. Samuel Gompers was the face of organized labor. He once took a young Theodore Roosevelt, then a state legislator on a guided tour of the other side of Roosevelt's native city, through the tenements and sweat shops that awakened the future president's conscience. Gompers, drawing on his nearly forty years in office, beat Lewis two to one. Some UMWA delegates, including Illinois district president Frank Farrington, voted against him, something Lewis would not soon forget or forgive. Little other than his driving ambition could explain why Lewis had attempted an all but impossible play. Lewis' own explanation later in life was that he "ran against Gompers for

1. From the Earth

the presidency of the AF of L in 1921 because a number of unions were sickened by Gompers depending upon the federal administration. They could not stomach the reverent awe which he had in his heart for presidents."[6] Lewis now began drafting new plans for his union and the labor contracts that were set to expire both for the benefit of the members but also to protect his base of power in organized labor. He also waged an open war with Farrington, who would fight back punch for punch.

A preview of the looming violence came in the copper mines of Butte, Montana, in 1917. In June an accident killed 168 miners. Union organizer Frank Little of the Industrial Workers of the World (IWW), a veteran activist of workers in many industries Little and the IWW tried to organize all workers into "one big union." Little attacked the war as well as the mining companies calling American troops "scabs in uniforms." On August 1, six masked men grabbed him from his hotel room, dragged him behind a car and lynched him off the side of a bridge. More than ten thousand lined the streets of Butte for his funeral. No one was arrested for the murder and Frank Little took his place as a radical martyr.

Mass violence marred the years after the Great War. Some outbreaks were the outgrowth of white supremacy directed against blacks. Others grew out of labor disputes. In 1919, black sharecroppers met in Elaine, Arkansas, to band together to negotiate better prices for their cotton, bypassing the white landowners who kept them in a perpetual struggle to survive. At the meeting, one white man intending to break up the meeting was killed and another wounded. During the next three days, thousands of whites invaded the countryside killing blacks. The exact number of African Americans killed is unknown. Some researchers put the number as low as 20, others as high as 826, but most historians estimate the deaths in the 100–237 range. Five whites were killed, which led the establishment to characterize the massacre as a "Negro uprising," while suppressing news of the number of innocent black people murdered. No whites were arrested but twelve blacks accused of killing whites faced charges. Six of them were tried under conditions so biased that the U.S. Supreme Court in the landmark case *Moore v. Dempsey* overturned the convictions. The six defendants fled Arkansas before they were retried. (To mark the centennial of the massacre authorities dedicated a memorial tree and marker. The tree was cut down and the marker vandalized.)

The true story of the Elaine Massacre was largely unknown, but the Tulsa, Oklahoma, riot in 1921 could not be hidden. Unlike the sharecroppers, blacks in Tulsa built the prosperous neighborhood of Greenwood often called the "Negro Wall Street." An African American bootblack was accused of assaulting a white elevator operator. By the standards of the day, the word rape was rarely if ever used in public or in newspapers, so the assault accusation often meant more than it does today. An armed white mob appeared at the jail demanding the suspect. A group of armed black citizens also appeared to protect him. War broke out between the races, but unlike in Elaine or East St. Louis, black people fought back. While certainly in the hundreds, the number of killed and wounded the next two days is unknown and probably never will be known. What was certain is that 35 square blocks of Greenwood were destroyed, leaving more than 10,000 blacks homeless. Under the eye of the national media city officials tried to blame African Americans for the violence and destruction. The Greenwood neighborhood never recovered and remains a scar on Tulsa.

As often as it was a matter of white and black violent outbreaks were about green, particularly in disputes between unions and management. In 1920 in Matewan, West Virginia, tensions between miners trying to unionize and coal operators supported by paid guards and the state government grew increasingly violent. On May 19 detectives from the Baldwin-Felts agency arrived in town to evict miner families from houses owned by the Stone Mountain Coal company. The outsiders were met by pro-union police chief Sid Hatfield and Mayor Cabell Testerman on their way out of Matewan. Both sides had arrest warrants for the others. Lured downtown, a gunfight broke out leaving seven detectives including two brothers of the agency's head and the mayor and two miners dead in the street. The gunfight was seen as a rare victory for the miners and Hatfield became a folk hero. Everyone arrested for the murders was acquitted.

Hatfield faced trial in a neighboring county. Appearing on the steps of the courthouse in August 1921, with his wife, the widow of the mayor he married two weeks after Testerman's death, and another couple Hatfield was assassinated under orders of the T.L. Felts to avenge his brothers' murders. The infuriated miners with the help of the UMWA began assembling an organized armed force. Despite pleas from union leaders the miner army started marching towards Matewan. The 13,000 troops were met by a force of sheriff deputies, mine guards and volunteers, many taking up position on Blair Mountain. While the battle raged, private airplanes dropped pipe bombs on the miners, causing no damage. After federal troops arrived to put down the conflict, the miners gave up and laid down their arms. Many miners were indicted but almost none

1. From the Earth

were convicted. At one trial the defendants brought an unexplored pipe bomb dropped by the coal operators. Under the spotlight of the nation's newspapers the Matewan Massacre and the Battle of Blair Mountain (events later portrayed in the 1987 film *Matewan*) coal miners across the country learned they could fight back with few consequences. Soon the lessons, both good and bad, of Matewan and Blair Mountain, would be applied by another group of miners in another, pro-union, part of America.

Across the ocean in 1921, British coal miners staged a national strike for better wages. It was an object lesson for America fearing a strike at home. Coal reserves soon dropped, forcing railroads to cut out service altogether on Sundays and cutting back on other days. Residents were limited to 28 pounds of coal a week and daylight savings time was increased by two hours to save coal-fueled electricity for lighting. The Newmarket meeting, a crown jewel of horse racing, was cancelled until gasoline-based transportation replaced the rail transportation to the track. The shortage of coal soon began shutting down factories. Soon department stores ran out of goods that were moved by rail. Workers throughout the British economy were laid off or had their workdays reduced. Businesses tried to import coal, literally bringing coal to New Castle, but the effort was hampered by the rail unions refusal to haul foreign coal coupled with a refusal of miners' union in other European countries to work on coal slated for export to the United Kingdom. The strike ended only after other unions voting by a narrow margin refused to go out in support.

News of the British miners' strike and the disruption to the economy was extensively reported in America including the *Literary Digest*, a widely read magazine of the time. In the same issue reporting on the British coal strike was an advertisement from the Consolidation Coal Company urging industrial buyers to stock up on coal "carefully prepared." "You can insist on clean coal in a time of ample production," the ad read. "You can refuse anything else. But when coal shortages come, you may be glad to get 'anything that is black,'" The ad encouraged buyers to stockpile their coal pile before the next shortage. In the same issue of the *Literary Digest* above an ad for a school for "subnormal children" were two ads for the Colorado School of Mines and the Michigan College of Mines and their four year degree offerings urging prospective students to enter a "wide and profitable field, not overcrowded."

The Herrin Massacre of 1922

In March that same year another figure history has tried to forget was inaugurated president. Until Donald Trump, Warren G. Harding was widely considered to be the worst president in American history. His brief time in office will forever be associated with the Teapot Dome scandal which did not come to light until after his death and with his reputation as a shallow, dim political hack more interested in drinking and womanizing than governing. Part of his reputation is well deserved but the worst of it is an exaggeration created in part by Harding's self-deprecating humor and insecurities.

"The only thing I really worry about is that I am sometimes very much afraid that I am going to be nominated and elected." Harding wrote to a friend in 1919.[7] "That is an awful thing to contemplate." In his hometown of Marion, Ohio, Harding grew up under the rumor that he was of mixed race. His father-in-law openly called him a "nigger." His slow, steady rise in Ohio politics and the newspaper business opened forums for speechmaking and editorial writing. Harding dismissed his statements as "bloviating," flowery, hollow assemblies of words which H.L. Mencken described as "dogs barking idiotically through endless nights." Harding's inaugural address was he wrote "rumble and bumble. It is flap and doodle. It is balder and dash."[8] Harding, Mencken wrote, had "the face of a moving-picture actor" but only "the intelligence of a respectable agricultural implement dealer." Mencken had no better opinion of Harding's Democratic opponent, David Cox, in 1920. Cox, who brought his young running mate Franklyn D. Roosevelt into the national

President Warren G. Harding, ca. 1910 (Library of Congress).

1. From the Earth

spotlight, had "a gift for bamboozling the boobs." William McAdoo, Wilson's son-in-law and secretary of the treasury, attacked Harding's speeches as "an army of pompous phrases moving over the landscape in search of an idea. Sometimes these meandering words actually capture a straggling thought and bear it triumphantly, a prisoner in their midst, until it died of servitude and over work."[9]

Harding liked to drink and play poker with his friends even in the White House despite both pleasures being illegal, but he showed up on time for work every morning. He had at least one extramarital affair but his reputation as an out of control womanizer is unjustified. He and First Lady Florence opened the White House to the arts and science communities including Albert Einstein and Madam Curie. Harding was considered handsome and popular by the newly enfranchised women voters in the 1920 election. "He was about as handsome a man as I ever saw," his fellow senator James Watson remembered, "and he had one of those affidavit faces whose very appearance carried confidence, and withal he was a magnificent figure."[10] Harding was a man of his times in a nation looking for normalcy to heal the scars of the Great War and the drama of the Wilson administration. President Harding demanded little from the American people and they demanded little from him. "If there is anything wrong with the White House job, it is the inability to be a human being," said Harding who remained very much a fallible human.[11]

As a newspaper publisher in Marion, Harding had good relations with his union employees. In the 1920 presidential election Socialist Eugene Debs received one million votes as he campaigned from a cell in a federal prison, including from Oak Park, Illinois, first time voter Ernest Hemingway. His words in a 1917 speech in Canton, Ohio, "if war is right let it be declared by the people. You who have your lives to lose, you certainly above all others have the right to decide the momentous issue of war and peace," were enough to convict him under the Wilson administration's persecution of dissent, however mild. Millions signed petitions for his release, the pages linked together in one long scroll wound around a large spool for delivery to the White House. Harding pardoned Debs, securing his release on December 25, 1921, and inviting him for a visit at the White House. Harding said he heard "men in Congress say worse" than the words pronounced by Debs.[12] Debs, Harding said, "had never been guilty of any overt act; that he never countenanced destruction of government by force, and that probably I could persuade him to become a factor in contributing to tranquility throughout the land." When Debs arrived at the White House, Harding shook his hand saying "I've heard so damned much about you Mr. Debs, that I am very glad to meet you personally." The coming year would present a much harder test of Harding's congenial relations with organized labor.

2

The Liveliest Place in Southern Illinois

At the start of the 1920s, the booming town of Herrin in Williamson County was enjoying the best of times. Williamson County is in the heart of southern Illinois, the region long known as Little Egypt or just Egypt because its delta shaped land between the Mississippi and Ohio rivers was reminiscent of the Nile river delta to the early pioneers schooled in the Bible with a dash of the classics. The southernmost tip, untouched by the glaciers that ground most of the rest of the state into flat prairies reaching to the horizon, was and is a spectacular land of hills and hollows, towering exposed rocks covered in dense forests. Its beauty yielded little but a hard life for the settlers. Further north the land flattened, inviting a not much easier life squeezing a living out of the soil.

Herrin had the mixed blessing of being surrounded by the some of the richest coal fields in the world.[1] Before the coal mines opened Williamson County was a hard scrabble farming region first settled in the early 1800s by a large number of families from Kentucky and Tennessee who brought the South with them, naming the county for their former home county in Tennessee. The area maintained other ties to the South: in the presidential contests of 1860 and 1864 Abraham Lincoln lost the county both times. From the first Williamson County acquired a well-deserved reputation as a violent place. A feud raged in the county in the mid–19th century originating in part from leftover tensions of the Civil War and in part from a dispute over a card game. The tangled and complex story of the feud, known as the Bloody Vendetta, involving various alliances of families was the Hatfields and McCoys without the moonshine humor.[2]

Including the deaths from the Bloody Vendetta between 1839 and 1876 the thinly populated county recorded 285 murders and 495 assaults

The Herrin Massacre of 1922

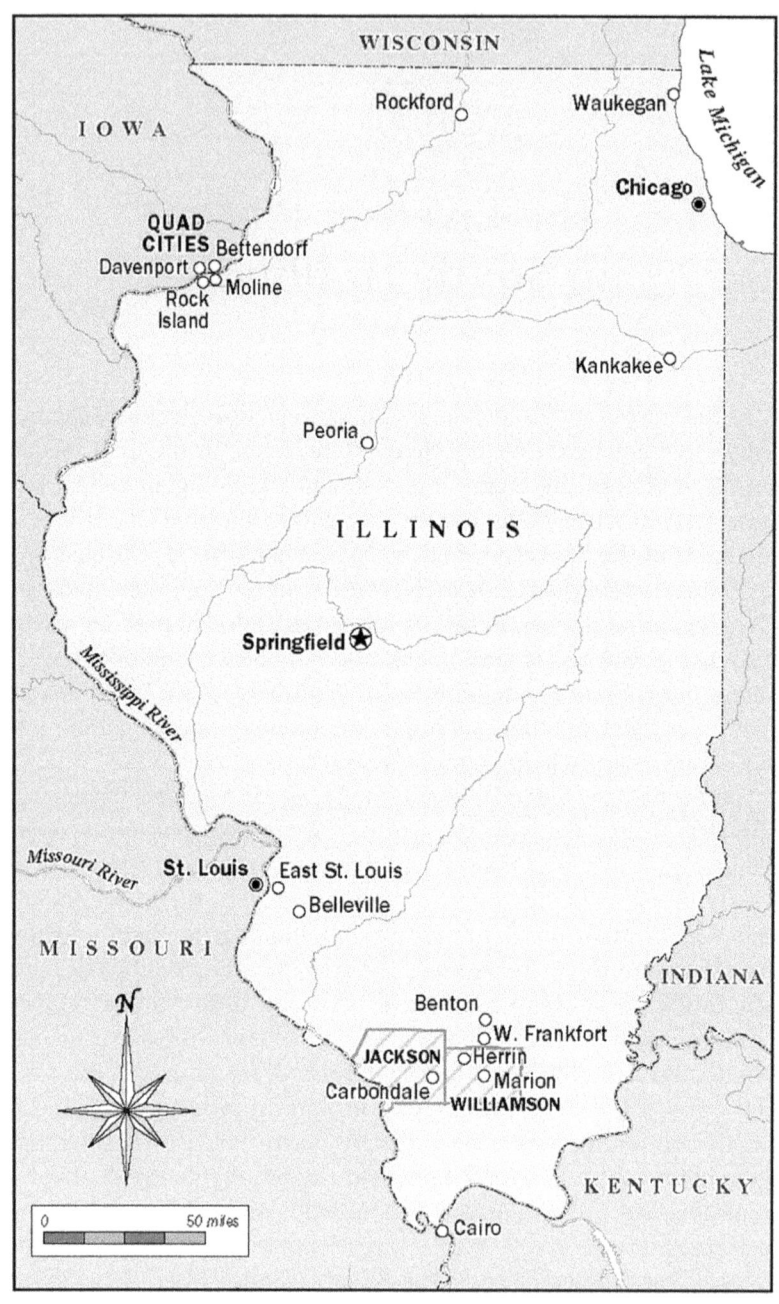

Map of Illinois, detailing the area surrounding Herrin and Marion.

2. The Liveliest Place in Southern Illinois

with a deadly weapon. Blood and violence were breed into the fabric of the region and its residents.

The most productive farmland in Illinois lay further north leaving those who remained behind in Egypt with a stern challenge. With the population shift power in Illinois moved northward as well taking the state capitols from Kaskaskia in southern Illinois to Vandalia, and then to Springfield. As if to emphasize its decline the first state capitol in Kaskaskia was swept into the Mississippi River along with almost everything else in the town and making the area an island cut off from the state it once controlled. Economic power shifted north as well eventually turning the small lakeside settlement named Chicago after the Native American name for the wild onions that grew there into a metropolitan giant.

It took some time to realize that there was more wealth under the soil in southern Illinois than there was on top of it. Coal was first discovered in Williamson County in 1869 by Laban Carter, namesake of the village of Carterville. The St. Louis & Big Muddy Coal Company opened a mine near Carterville in 1890, one of many that appeared in the coal rich region. Eight years later, the mine became the focal point of a strike that would end in violence, and a number of lessons, learned and unlearned, for labor, management and the government.

The miners, led by the fledgling United Mine Workers of America, went out on strike, and mine manager Sam T. Brush appealed to the members to disregard their union, openly paying a group of miners a $1,000 cash bribe to call a meeting of the strikers together.[3] The union miners refused to give in. Brush then contacted his son who was waiting in Jellico, Tennessee, to bring up the black strikebreakers he had already recruited. The African Americans were brought into Carterville on a special train on May 20 and delivered to the mine.

For a week tensions mounted. A crowd of some 1,500 union miners from across Illinois gathered in the small town. The sheriff and a number of newly deputized officers faced down the mob and sent the union supporters home. The strike was broken and about 100 miners reapplied for their old jobs, working alongside black miners.

In his first-person account, Brush claimed that three employees came to him asking for increased wages after promising they were not union members. He gave them the raises and then discovered that they were in fact union members now claiming he had made a binding contract with the union. Brush fired the three workers and another strike was called. The white miners and a few blacks left but most of the blacks stayed on the

The Herrin Massacre of 1922

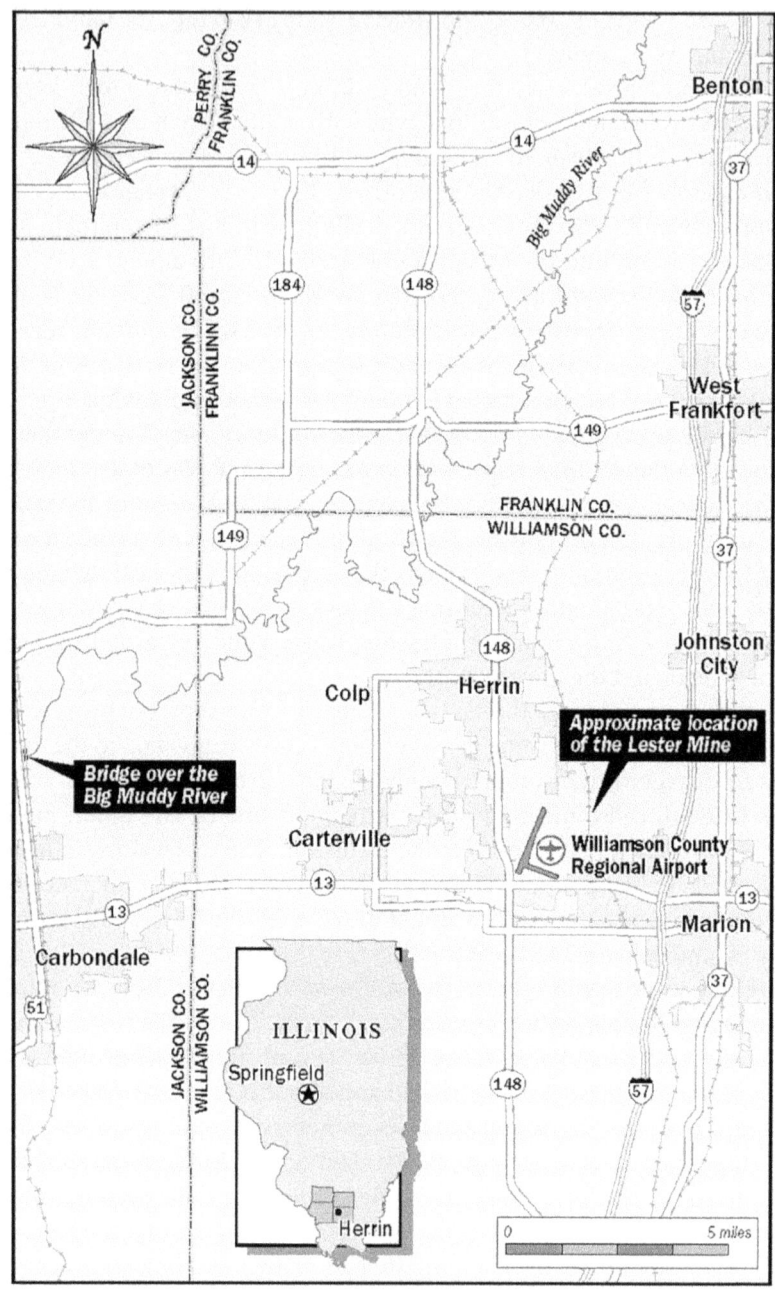

Map of Williamson County and surrounding counties.

2. The Liveliest Place in Southern Illinois

job. Brush considered bringing in more men from Tennessee but instead engaged a number of African Americans expelled from a mine in Pana, Illinois, following another attempt to break a miners' strike. The train bringing the strikebreakers was fired upon near Carterville on June 30. One black woman, the wife of a strikebreaker, was killed and some twenty wounded.

The following day the union miners and guards exchanged fire at the mine. The company housing for the black miners was set on fire. The governor immediately sent troops to the area, some of them Spanish American War veterans. The units temporarily calmed the conflict. The militia stayed until September, as the black strikebreakers huddled in the mine and the white union members waited in town.

On Sunday, September 17, a few black miners ventured into Carterville's train station. What happened next is disputed, the mine owner later claiming the black strikebreakers were unarmed and that some were on their way to attend church in nearby Marion "as the colored people have no church in Carterville" and the miners claiming the strikebreakers were armed and started shooting first. In any event, five of the black strikebreakers were killed. The accused white miners were arrested, tried and acquitted.

Brush, writing after the event, had only learned one lesson from the carnage he brought to Carterville "While the mine owners have been assured of protection from the county and State, they have not found that such protection was afforded until disaster came, and as a result, have not depended entirely upon such precautions, but have provided arms of their own in sufficient quantity and of the best quality to be used by their trusted employees in case of emergency. This fact being known by the strikers, has prevented them from coming close enough to the mines to destroy the property." The Carterville Riot, as it came to called, was in minds of everyone later involved in the events in Herrin, whether they had participated in it, held it as a childhood memory or had learned of it in endless retellings around the dinner table or schoolyard.

The lesson learned by the workers of Williamson County went beyond a union that stood up for them in Carterville. The union contract brought better wages and working conditions, and better lives for their families. There were no company-controlled towns or payments in script in Southern Illinois. Coal mining was still a dirty and dangerous way of life but under the union they were treated like men with some respect and pride. It showed in the nightly competition among miners' wives to put the brightest shine on their husbands' lunch pails which came home blackened with coal. The fact that despite continuing outbreaks of violence and disastrous mining accidents the union miners could expect to return to their homes at the end of a workday was more than their fathers and grandfathers could have expected. They were never going back to the way things were before the union.

The UMWA represented all of the miners in Williamson County, roughly 15,000 by the start of the 1920s. With membership came political power and every candidate for office knew he had to have the support of the union miners to win. Many public officials were either former miners or active union members. The local chamber of commerce, called the Greater Marion Association, broke off its affiliation with the national and state organizations because of the latter's anti-union stances. In 1921, A.T. Pace, a local union leader who would soon become the mayor of Herrin, wrote that the members had "unswerving loyalty and true devotion to their country "describing them as "conservative, loyal to their Government and one hundred percent American." Most miners, he said, owned their own homes.

During World War I, approximately 1,500 Williamson County union miners left to serve in the armed forces, some never to return, and those remaining increased coal production to help defeat the Kaiser while maintaining strong support for bond drives and charity fundraising. During the war UMWA officials intervened to settle a labor dispute with the Coal Belt electric trolley that ran between Marion, Herrin and Carterville, a vital transportation link for area miners and residents. Coal companies published honor rolls of employees who served in the war. On the surface, at least, it was a rare period of harmony.

Herrin was by comparison to Williamson County and southern Illinois a cosmopolitan, progressive community. Named for an early settler David Herrin, the small village was founded in 1898 grew to 1,876 when incorporated in 1900. Ten years later it had reached 6,864, and by 1917 a special census found 10,408 residents. By the early 1920s, the population was at least 11,000 and growing. Herrin boasted it was "the largest soft coal mining city in the United States, situated within the whistle sound of thirty-five shipping mines."

More than a thousand residents were foreign born, mostly from Italy as recorded in the 1920 census. For the most part the native and foreign born coexisted peacefully. That general harmony had exploded in 1915

2. The Liveliest Place in Southern Illinois

in nearby Johnson City with the lynching of a Sicilian immigrant miner named Joe Strando.

Strando was accused of killing farmer Edward Chapman and wounding his daughter. A mob dragged Strando out of jail to a railroad coal shed and hung him briefly before letting him down, demanding he confess to the murder. Strando recovered his breath and confessed that he and another Italian, Joe Bingo, had committed the crimes. Strando was hoisted up again and left to slowly strangle as the mob watched. His dead body was left hanging for hours. A group of armed immigrant miners, including some from Herrin, formed to avenge Strando. The two mobs stood ready for a fight until the governor deployed the state militia to Johnson City. Six years later, another Sicilian miner, Settino de Santis, before his own legal hanging for murdering two boys, confessed he had killed Chapman.

Alongside the Protestant, mainly Baptist, churches in Herrin were Catholic churches and Italian focused schools and associations like Giuseppe Garibaldi Society, the Lombard Society and Court Cristoforo Colombo branch of the Foresters of America. African Americans had a lower profile in Herrin, but in the context of the times and the country not an altogether negative one. In 1915 the Williamson County Miners' Improvement Society walked out of a Herrin hotel after it refused service to a black member. Herrin was large enough to be noticed by the outside world. In 1921 the Chicago Cubs played the St. Louis Giants in Herrin and the following year the Detroit Tigers played a semipro team from the area.

After the war, the Williamson County War History Society marked the contributions of its citizens and community by publishing a 393-page book with the photos and brief biographies of almost everyone from the county who served in the military, including, like the military itself, a segregated section on "colored" soldiers. The book, edited by newspaper man Hal Trovillian, also turned its focus upon the folks and firms back home. Herrin prided itself on being the "best wage city in the Mississippi Valley, furnishing a greater number of working days the year around and a higher wage for the working man than any other city in the state and probably the Middle West."

Herrin also took pride that it "has always been called a young man's town, because the young man has opportunities here to an apparent, greater degree than in other cities that boast of years and learned and aged men." Coal mining companies took special note in rolls of honor of all of their employees who left for the military while, with justification, congratulating themselves for keeping up supplies of coal for the

The Herrin Massacre of 1922

war effort. In 1916, a year before America entered the war, Williamson County mines produced almost eight million tons of coal or 930 tons per miner. Two years later, responding to the increased demand for coal, the county produced more than 11 million tons or 1,170 tons per worker. The soldiers and sailors "did not serve their country any more patriotically and unselfishly, than the man who stayed at home and toiled in the mines to produce the coal that was so much needed."

The Herrin Improvement Association, "the common council where the laboring man, the banker, the business and professional man meet on the same level," boasted that Herrin had thirty miles of "granitoid sidewalks" and "an adequate sewer system that cost $60,000." After the doughboys came home, the Association threw a celebration and banquet for the local heroes.

The people of Herrin had almost everything they could want in their own business district. Herrin residents could buy the latest in clothing from the Kahn Store, "Outfitter for Man, Woman and Child," or the Good Luck Clothing Company, M.P. Zwick, Sam Susman, Yuill Brothers Mercantile Company or the Lombard Society Store, which was owned by the Italian community but open for everyone. The latest styles in shoes were offered at the McMinn-Jones Shoe Company. Dressed in their best people could attend the Hippodrome Theatre, a 1,500-seat theater that made Herrin "the capital city in Theaterdom by the high class attractions both in pictures, artists and plays offered." Or they could stroll over to the Spezia Confectionary, "a popular rendezvous for the younger set," or go to John Maurizol's or Frank Traveggia's parlors.

Herrin had two large hotels with cafes, the European, founded by Italian Louis Dell-Ern, and the Jefferson. The Herrin Supply Store proclaimed, "We sell everything under the sun." The Bracy-North Hardware Company, the Sunnyside Supply Company and the Southside Supply Company also sold hardware and other goods, including guns. The Cash Store kept prices low and H.A. Tate was ready to sell motorists a Maxwell, Nash, Dodge Brothers or Jordan automobile. The Herrin Ice and Cold Storage Company was responsible for preventing the "ice famines in the hottest seasons of the year" and operated a "sanitary ice cream factory." The Howard & Casey Wholesale Grocers manufactured the "HO-CA-CO" line of foods and the "SERV-US" brand of coffee, and the Blue Grass Butter Company made Jersey brand butter, which may have been available locally at Sam Warner & Co., Henry Fowler, B.E. Hamilton or the Sizemore Company grocery stores.

2. The Liveliest Place in Southern Illinois

People in Herrin had their choice of drug stores among L.V. Cline and R.A. Karr, but the Holland Drug Company also carried the "Claxionola talking machine." Herrin took special pride in pointing to the O.K. Shining Parlor run by Greek brothers Nick and Louis Lockus who were "good citizens and are examples of the world's greatest melting pot that the United States has been proud to claim," and to Lee Hand's Laundry who "is quite Americanized and in the war did his bit in all war funds and charities." Argentine born Pete Cardani, Herrin's most successful building contractor, was noted for his "agreeableness with labor." The small city had two newspapers, the *News* and the *Journal*. Behind the public face presented by the Herrin business community there were a number of speakeasies and gambling dens openly but invisibly operating while leaving few records to history, which would later in the decade fuel another round of violence in the county. Without irony, Herrin was, in its own opinion "known everywhere as the liveliest place in Southern Illinois."

3

Overburden

As John L. Lewis calculated the next moves for the union, a new mine opened near Herrin. In September, the Southern Illinois Coal Company, owned by William J. Lester of Cleveland, Ohio, began operations. It was a strip mine, a relatively new form of mining, at the time accounting for less than one percent of coal production in Illinois. The process involves removing the layers of soil and rock, called the overburden, that cover the coal seam.[1] The exposed coal deposits were excavated and loaded with greater safety and less cost than underground mines. The disadvantage—propaganda of the coal industry notwithstanding—is that strip mining leaves a permanent scar on the land and that even the best efforts of reclamation look like a botched operation performed by a back-alley plastic surgeon. Strip mining would leave its mark long after the coal was gone across the landscape of vast parts of America. The Lester mine would leave the deepest scar of all.

William Junius Lester was a civil engineering graduate of Cornell, class of 1896.

A native of Fredonia, New York, Lester worked as an engineer for mining operations in Colorado and Pennsylvania before starting his own company. Solidly built, bald and wearing wire rim glasses, he looked every inch the stereotype of a businessman of the decade, someone who could have stepped out of the pages of a Sinclair Lewis novel.

Lester bought an 80-acre tract of land from Ed Crenshaw that had been the Chenoweth family farm. Under the soil, 10 to 25 feet below the surface, was a rich vein of coal waiting to be removed. To mine it Lester, brought in two Bucyrus steam shovels, enormous machines like the ones used to dig the Panama Canal.[2] In addition he had a rail spur built into the property, and brought in a locomotive, tank cars, switches and a railroad scale. The mine had a fleet of seven "camp cars," a newer Dodge, a gasoline truck and a team of horses and a wagon. He built a

3. Overburden

700-foot long dam to create a 16-acre pond needed to supply the water to wash the coal before loading, and built a compound bringing together a blacksmith shop, machine shop, electric sub-station, pumphouse, houses to store powder and oil, and an office on site. Altogether, he had invested about $250,000 of his own money in the operation.

The UMWA miners operating the shovels began removing the overburden, piling it into slopes on both sides of a broad avenue-like corridor of exposed coal about half a mile long. In November, the mine began its first shipments, loading the coal on rail cars on a spur built into the property by the Burlington Railroad. The seven-foot-thick seam of high grade coal was rich and business was good.

The fledgling company employed UWMA miners without an argument but Lester's background in mining had involved non-union mines and mining operations where weaker unions were broken. The 1920s glorified the businessman as the new American icon. (Later in 1925 a best-selling book, *The Man Nobody Knows* by Bruce Fairchild Barton, recast Jesus as the world's greatest business executive.) In the decade that proclaimed that the business of America is business and glorified individualism, Lester, like many in the business community, had an inborn contempt for organized labor. As a stranger to the culture of southern Illinois, he apparently did not understand the hard-won accomplishments and fierce reverence of the union in the region.

Through the end of 1921 into the beginning of 1922 as the deadline for a new coal contract approached with little realistic hope on either side that a strike could be averted. Harding continued to urge a settlement to avoid a strike but neither side was willing to budge. Lewis was intent upon making up ground lost during the war and coal operators were equally intent on holding the line against increased wages and benefits.

Lewis' plan was challenged by a new dispute in Kansas under the leadership of Alex Howat.[3] Scottish native Howat had entered the coal mines when he was 10 years old. By his 22nd birthday he was a union officer. In 1906 he was elected president of the Kansas district. When he was falsely accused of taking bribes from the mine operators he stepped down, cleared his name, and resumed the presidency at the next election. Howat defied the wartime freeze on strikes that lead the Kansas legislature to enact the Industrial Relations Act, which outlawed strikes, picketing and boycotts and forced all labor disputes into a Court of Industrial Relations. Howat refused to obey the law and paid for it multiple times in jail. In

The Herrin Massacre of 1922

1921, he led a wildcat strike in defiance of Lewis' orders and was removed from office.

At the September 1921 convention in Indianapolis, Howat, despite support from Frank Farrington's Illinois District 12 and other Midwestern delegations, unsuccessfully challenged his expulsion. In Kansas that December, the "Amazon Army," a marching crowd of an estimated 6,000 women, confronted strikebreakers and mine guards.[4] The mothers, wives, and sisters of the striking miners faced down the state militia and hired gunmen in a series of confrontations. Armed only with American flags and red pepper they planned to throw in the face of strikebreakers, the women were fired upon but did not back down. Forty-nine of the women were arrested before the protest ended.

Howat and his expelled supporters appeared at the 1922 convention but were barred from speaking. During the turmoil, a small, elderly woman known as Mother Jones, the Miner's Angel, took the podium. No one would dare stop the legendary figure who had devoted most of her life to the struggles of working people on the picket lines, the backroads, the desperate camps of starving children and the constant and often violent fight for the union. She began by reminding the assembled miners that "everywhere the electric current touches it is notifying the world what you are doing here today."

"I have known Alex Howat for twenty years," she said, "and while I have not always agreed with Alex, I want to make this statement to the audience and the world. That is my desire to have a million Alex Howats in the nation to fight the battles of the workers. He has fought for his men and he has fought that damnable law that the Governor of Kansas put on the statute books to enslave the workers. He fought it nobly and he was ready to go to death for it, and because he did he was put in jail and denounced."[5] Mother Jones compared Howat to abolitionist John Brown and predicted his monument would become a shrine. She read a letter from woman in Kansas, presumably one member of the Amazon Army, praising Howat's fight for the miners' families.

After a few additional calls for action, she left the stage. She would never return. Lewis unofficially purged her from the UMWA, silencing her voice before the events looming on the horizon. Lewis had secured his authority, but the sympathetic example of Alex Howat and the Kansas fighters was fresh in the minds of rank and file miners.

Another fallout from the Alex Howat dispute was the fueling of the ongoing fight between Lewis and Frank Farrington, president of Dis-

3. Overburden

trict 12 of the UMWA, covering the entire state of Illinois. Farrington had already clashed with Lewis over the war era agreements, and Farrington had exposed three of Lewis' brothers who were stealing funds from a local union in Illinois. In a May 1922 convention in Muskogee, Oklahoma, Farrington said, "I am not trying to destroy the international union but I am trying to destroy John L. Lewis, the man who is doing more to destroy the United Mine Workers of America, than any other man I know of." Lewis, Farrington said, "will not have my support until as long as he is using the power of his position to crucify men who won't jump through the hoop every time he snaps his fingers and tells them to do it."

A month before the coal strike deadline, the pro labor *American Flint* published an anonymous poem entitled "Pretty Rotten" that should have served as a warning to the strikebreakers, called scabs by union members, before traveling from Chicago to southern Illinois.

> They said that he was scabby
> And they threw him in the creek
> But he poisoned all the pollywogs
> And made the fishes sick.
>
> Then they threw him in the sewer
> Said "We know what we're about,"
> But the sewer rats protested
> So they had to throw him out
>
> The chased him to the tall grass,
> To live among the snakes:
> But a snake said "Take him out,
> That guy gives me the shakes."
>
> So then they had a meeting,
> And all began to blab:
> They decided he could go to hell!
> The best place for a scab.[6]

The union and its supporters were not the only ones preparing for a fight. The Illinois Coal Operators Association published a public relations booklet titled "What is Behind the Wage Contract with Illinois Miners?" to gain the public's support in the looming strike. "Twenty five years ago, the coal operators of Illinois, impelled by the necessity of securing peace with mine labor, and stimulated by the hope of securing guarantees for the greater continuity of mine operations adopted the system of negotiation wage contracts by collective bargaining. It must be admitted that the methods then adopted and since followed, have not achieved success." The booklet followed with a long litany of grievances against the union, aimed at the public which could soon feel the coal shortage firsthand. The Consolidated Coal Company ran ads in consumer magazines like the *Literary Digest* reassuring the public that along with the 15 million tons of coal it was producing it had another two billion tons in reserve. Still, fears of a shortage, or "coal famine" as some newspapers deemed it, continued to build.

Certainly, William Lester knew, as did everyone else, that a strike was looming and with it would come higher prices for the coal the country needed to function. At what point he decided to break the strike is not known. But while other operators prepared to ride out the stoppage, Lester was making plans to defy it.

In February, Sam T. Brush died, a reminder of the bad old days of labor violence in Williamson County that seemed a thing in the distant past. As winter turned to spring, the union and the industry prepared for action. Large users of coal stockpiled as much supply as they could. Lewis called a national strike to begin on April 1. Before and after the deadline, Farrington threatened to sign a separate agreement with the operators. Union mines across the country shut down, including the forty-four large and small operations in Williamson County, from Peabody Coal to the Pratt Coal Company. The Lester mine shut down as well. There were no picket lines outside of the mines—no one would dare try to break the strike.

In the April primary, incumbent sheriff Melvin Thaxton won the Republican nomination for county treasurer, marking the countdown to the end of his law enforcement career. The biggest news that month was the acquittal of Roscoe "Fatty" Arbuckle, once the most popular movie star in America, for the manslaughter of Virginia Rappe. Even with the not guilty verdict, his films were banned, and his career ended.

Lester was facing a substantial chance of losing his investment if the strike persisted.

At some point he made an arrangement with the local union and its representative Hugh Willis to keep up the maintenance of the equipment and continue removal of the overburden with the strict condition that no coal be loaded or removed from the mine. Several other mines in the county also made arrangements with the union to complete construction projects already in progress, and to maintain pumps and other equipment to prevent flooding in the deep mine shafts and tunnels, again with the same condition. This arrangement was beneficial to both sides,

3. Overburden

giving Lester an advantage to ship coal as soon as the strike ended when market prices would be at their highest and giving the union members more weeks of paid work during the strike. Although there is no evidence to support the accusation, it would be naive to believe that money was not passed under the table, a view shared by many at the time. Such arrangements were not uncommon and there was a tradition of collusion between unions and operators who planned and carried out local strikes which would drive up the price of coal enough to allow the mine to pay increased wages out of the windfall. Whatever the truth, the mine kept working removing the overburden.

Lester had an interest in another nearby strip mine with Charles Hamilton. Like Lester, Hamilton was an outsider, but he had lived in southern Illinois long enough to understand the realities of the area. In April, Lester approached him with the idea that he could break the strike and work the mine. Hamilton flatly told him it would be "absolutely impossible" and that he didn't want to know anything else about it. Hamilton made it clear to Lester that their jointly owned operation would not attempt to break the strike.

Sometime that April, Lester brought into his operation notorious strikebreaker C.K. McDowell to be the superintendent and manager. Claude Klein McDowell appeared on the streets of Marion with a pistol on his hip. Because he lost a leg in a mine war in Kansas, a miner later recalled, some called him "Peggy," a cruel reference to his artificial leg. McDowell, however, was not the kind of person to inspire sympathy. As he swaggered about town, he openly boasted that he had broken unions before in Colorado and Kansas and could do it again.

Around that time, as residents later remembered, crates arrived at the depot for the Lester mine. Later it was determined the crates contained two machine guns, rifles, a large supply of ammunition and tear gas grenades. One shipment of weapons from Hibbard, Spencer, Bartlett & Co. cost $1,623. The weapons were stockpiled at the mine office. The commissary stocked provisions worth between $3,000 and $4,000. New people began to appear at the mine. Few knew they were from the Hargrave Detective Agency in Chicago, hired thugs paid to break unions. Around that time, a public road running next to the property was blocked by a mound of earth, much to the annoyance of local residents. Reports of the blocked road and minor harassments by the guards working at the Lester mine began coming into the sheriff's office.

The Herrin Massacre of 1922

As the strike continued into June, the mine had uncovered about 60,000 tons of coal—at the rising market prices, worth about $250,000. The work of removing the overburden had reached an end point. Without warning, on June 13, Lester fired all of the union employees, ejecting them from the mine.

4

Detonators

William Lester's intentions quickly became clear. By June 15 he had moved strikebreakers into the mine along with the armed guards. Bunk cars and a commissary car to cook for the roughly fifty employees were pulled into place. On the following day, the operation loaded its first shipment of coal. A train crew flatly refused to enter the property and take away the sixteen cars filled with coal, but a second crew ordered by Lester agreed and hauled the shipment out of the area.

Those now inside of the mine had been recruited from Chicago to travel to far southern Illinois to work. Drawn from many ethnic groups, some of them were skilled operators of heavy machinery and railroads, some were unskilled laborers, a few were cooks. They had been recruited by the Bertrand Employment Agency with promises of room and board in addition to $9.50 a day in wages, $6.00 a day for the cooks. Nominally some of them were members of the Steam Shovel Men's Union, but unless they were delusional, they knew it was a sham and not a real union in any meaningful sense. President William Howard Taft was an honorary member, a distinction connected to the digging of the Panama Canal. "I believe in labor organizations, and if I were skilled enough I should apply for membership," he told a crowd in Mechanics Hall in Worcester, Massachusetts, in 1910. The union refused to merge with another construction union leading the American Federation of Labor to expel it in 1918. The supposed union that appeared in Herrin was more of a façade for the owner than a true labor union.

Five or six men working in the Lester mine quit after the end of their first shift. Some of them, William Sneed later said, reported to the UMWA office to tell them they were not scabs and would not work under armed guards. Sneed said one mechanic from Chicago said when he informed McDowell he was quitting, the superintendent told him "the sooner you get off the grounds, the better." E.H. Renaud, in charge of the commissary,

The Herrin Massacre of 1922

plotted to leave with the truck going to pick up additional strikebreakers at the train station. They told him there wouldn't be room for him on the trip back. "I did not intend to tell them that I did not intend to come back."[1] Certainly the outsiders working in the mine so far from home knew they were strikebreakers, but it is likely that few of them realized the full extent of the danger they faced.

Perhaps they felt some comfort from the squad of armed guards surrounding them. They were under contract from the Hargraves Detective Agency. Sherman Holmes, a hired guard working under a 90 day contract, wrote a letter to his ex-wife Faye Koonce on the evening of June 19. Addressing her as "Mrs. Fay" Holmes wrote he was making $12 a day for sitting around with a rifle on his lap: "I have been here close by since June 9th. No doubt you will be surprised to learn I am Down here with a gang of Moonshiners. Ha! Ha! But the moonshine is Winchester Rifles & Field Guns. We are only waiting for them to start the Band playing. ... We haven't had much trouble here yet. But we are prepared for all that comes."[2]

Holmes told her about the machine guns and claimed there were 100 armed guards in the mine. "Give all my Foes & Friends my regards tell them I am here 8 Hour shift waiting for someone to stick their Head over the mountain or out of the woods. So as to give us a little practice to shoot at." He closed his letter to his ex: "I have a pal. He wants to know if there

Group photo of UMWA officials. *Top row, left to right:* **Herrin Mayor A.T. Pace; local union official Hugh Willis; William G. Davis; local union official Fox Hughes.** *Bottom row, left to right:* **State Senator George Cooper and union official William J. Sneed.**

4. Detonators

are any young chickens there. Some night when we get a Gallon of Real Moonshine we will take a Drive over.... We are not allowed off Company Mine Property at present."

Another guard was Patrick O'Rourke from Chicago. Born in Ireland, O'Rourke was part of one of the strongest Irish communities in the world. Chicago was then, as now, a city of neighborhoods. The Irish neighborhood O'Rourke called home was a tight knit community of a strong parish church and the corner saloon. The Irish worked the hardest jobs in the city, in the stockyards and the construction sites. Although the Irish had political power disproportionate to their numbers in Chicago, opening the police and fire departments and other patronage jobs to them, it was also a time when they were stereotyped as low, often intoxicated criminals. Employers routinely placed signs on their storefronts or factory gates: "No Irish Need Apply." When O'Rourke walked the streets of his city, the terms billy club and paddy wagon still had their original anti–Irish connotations. On the whole, his life, while different, was no easier that of any coal miner in southern Illinois.

The rifle-toting guards patrolled the boundaries of the property and at the crest of the fort-like mounds of earth set up machine gun emplacements overlooking the scraggly corn fields and woods. The local newspapers covered the developing story of imported workers and armed men matter of factly, the full danger of what was unfolding not yet apparent.

McDowell had moved out of his rented house in Marion and, after sending his wife to Lakewood, Ohio, moved into the strip mine. Secured inside the office McDowell told Lucian Tucker, a local businessman, "We came down here to work this mine, union or no union. We will work it with blood if necessary, and you can tell all of the Goddamned union men to stay away if they don't want trouble."[3]

His guards quickly antagonized the already inflamed people of the area by heavy handed bullying. Farmers soon noticed their crops and animals destroyed or stolen. One local resident would later testify that as he was picking berries near the mine, he felt a gun pressed to his body. "What the Goddamned hell are you doing here? Beat it, and Goddamned quick."[4]

Another pair of guards stopped a local driving on a public road by the mine. Pulling him out of his car one of the guards shouted, "He's a Goddamned son-of-a-bitching spy."[5] The pair beat the man and stole what little money he had on him. "If you ever cheep this I'll bump you off," one of the guards threatened. Toliver Nelson was stopped on a public road by some guards. One armed man wildly shouted, "I eats them alive. Kill him. Kill him. I likes 'em hot. I likes hot blood."[6] Even Deputy Sheriff Al Richardson was assaulted by the heavily armed Lester men, who told him, "We don't give a damn if you're the President of the United States; you move on."

Another group of armed men showed up at the home of 16-year-old Altha Davis, where she was alone with her seven-year-old sister.[7] "By God, we want some milk," the guards told her. She gave them buttermilk, but they demanded regular milk. As they drank, they asked Davis how old she was and if she went to the picture shows in town. After finishing their milk, the men left them alone.

A group of three friends out for ride were stopped by the guards.[8] Chris Karas, a waiter in a Marion restaurant, when questioned at gunpoint was so scared he could only point at his friend and sputter, "Ask this guy." One of the guards later struck him in the nose with the gun butt. On another occasion, three men were stopped on the public highway. They were forced at gunpoint to go to the mine office, surrounded by armed men. They were ordered to raise their arms over their head. When one of the men lowered his arms a little, McDowell hit him in the face. Another was grabbed and thrown across the room. "If you make one false move, I'll blow your head off," one of the armed men said.

McDowell finally ordered their release. "If any man makes a false move kill all three of them," the superintendent said. One of the armed men escorting them off the property said, "I will break your goddamned jaw." More than twenty people, including local women, would later testify that they were also abused by the guards.

W.M. Burton, a powder salesman, was stopped and assaulted by the guards as he tried to enter the mine to collect a bill.[9] Lester paid him and then showed him the arsenal he had collected. Burton asked Lester if he knew about the Brush mine and the deaths in the Carterville Riot. Lester said, "Our operation is different. We use less men and can pay a certain amount for protection, and if the shovel is blown up, we will get $800 a day insurance." McDowell approached the two and Lester said, "If McDowell doesn't make me $7,500 a day, I'll run him over the hill. Isn't that right, Mac?" McDowell nodded. "I've broken strikes before and I'll break this one," Lester said. As Burton was leaving, McDowell showed him a machine gun and told Burton, "Don't advertise this."

The intensity among union miners and their supports in Herrin and the region was building as well, but quietly and out of view. Word that scabs were working a mine and loading coal spread across the country-

4. Detonators

side. Newspapers in the area were openly on the union side since the beginning of the strike. (One newspaper, the *Marion Daily Republican*, ran a seven part series teaching out-of-work miners how to build a crystal radio.)[10] As strikebreakers were transported into the Lester mine, the local newspapers reported it unemotionally but the information only led to increased anger among their readers.

One resident stopped by the guards on the public road threatened to go to the State's Attorney in Marion. "You and the State's Attorney can go to hell," the guard replied.[11] Instead, State's Attorney Delos Duty went to the mine on Saturday morning, June 17, accompanied by Sheriff Melvin Thaxton and Deputies J.A. Shaffer and S.E. Storm (or Storme as it was often spelled in official reports and newspapers).

Duty was the rare office holder in Williamson County who had not worked in the mines. As a young man he tried to enlist in the Spanish American War, but his father would not sign the consent form. He earned a degree in pharmacy and opened a drug store in Marion in a two-story building bearing his name that still stands today. While working in the drug score he studied law by correspondence courses. He briefly served stateside during the war before returning home.

In 1920, Duty was elected state's attorney and prosecuted a murder case on his first day in office. Sheriff Thaxton had the more typical background as miner, with experience in farm work. He had been sheriff for four years and was running for county treasurer in the fall elections. Their car was stopped by guard William Cairns who demanded to know where they were going. "Who in the hell wants to know?" snapped Duty. After an argument, Cairns relented and agreed to take them inside. He stood on the car's running board as the four were escorted to the office. Cairns asked the party to stay in the car. "Don't you know who we are?" Duty said. "I am the state's attorney. This is the sheriff of the county and two of his deputies." Duty confronted McDowell with the accusations of harassment and violence against the public and demanded he remove the guards from the road. Duty also asked the superintendent to stop working the mine during the strike, advising him of the danger. McDowell agreed to remove the armed men but refused to stop work.

About the time Duty and Thaxton were confronting McDowell, Col. Sam Hunter of the Illinois National Guard in Springfield was reading an article in the *Chicago Tribune* that George Sutton, an aide in the governor's office, had handed him. Hunter, an insurance broker before the World War, rose from private to major in one year and was now assigned

Top center: **Sheriff Melvin Thaxton.** *Bottom, left to right:* **deputies John S. Layman, J.A. Schafer, and S.E. Storme.**

to personnel in the Illinois adjutant general's office. A one-paragraph story from Herrin, tacked on almost as an afterthought to the main story about Secretary of Commerce Herbert Hoover's meeting with coal producers, greatly alarmed Hunter. "Machine Guns to Guard Mine," read the

4. Detonators

headline over a brief item about weapons being brought in to protect the "miner's camp" when "attempts will be made to produce and ship coal." Hunter was a native of Perry County, which almost borders Williamson County. He knew exactly what the story meant, how dangerous the situation was and how badly it could end.

Col. Hunter's superior officer, Gen. Carlos Black, was at a camp in northern Illinois and his two immediate superiors were away. Governor Len Small was in Waukegan standing trial for corruption he alleged committed while he served as the state treasurer. Hunter tried unsuccessfully to reach Gen. Black, then called Duty. The situation, he learned from Duty, was worse than he feared. Upon his own authority, Hunter sent a telegram to Duty setting up a meeting the following day with Duty, Sheriff Thaxton and other parties from the union and the mine. Hunter also wired Major Robert Davis in Carbondale to join him on the trip to Marion.

Hunter and Davis arrived in Marion about 1:45 p.m. on Sunday, June 18. Within a few hours Hunter and Marion Police Officer W.A. Thorton drove to the Lester mine and met the usual armed reception. McDowell greeted Hunter with the request that the state send troops to protect the mine, with the promise that the paid guards would be let go. Hunter refused and told McDowell his thug tactics on the roads and the open breaking of the strike were menaces to the community. "You must open up these roads, disband your guards, and treat Uncle Sam and citizens here with respect," Hunter told McDowell.

McDowell bragged he had broken strikes at other mines and would not back done. "We know our business. We have money back of us and we are going to operate this mine as we please."[12] He also told Hunter that he had heard scattered gunshots but could not determine where they came from. Before leaving, Hunter said he would call for the sheriff to request troops if they were needed. Hunter pointed to the stockpile of firearms and ammunition, and asked McDowell what they were for. "This is being kept for ducks," said McDowell.

Back in Marion, Hunter listened to groups of angry miners walking the streets, promising violence if the mine did not close. Robert Tracy, an engineer at the mine operating the small locomotive on the grounds, found ten sticks of dynamite and two cans of black powder inside of the train's firebox. The following morning Hunter meet with Lester, Thaxton and Major Davis in Duty's office. Duty and Hunter both told Lester he was risking his life and his business if he continued operating. Lester brazenly demanded that the sheriff deputize ten or twenty of his guards. Hunter warned Lester in private that the sheriff would not intervene to protect him or his company and again implored him to stop. "I'll be damned if I will," Lester answered.

After the meeting broke up, Hunter phoned Gen. Black. The community, he told Black, was on the edge of a war. The sheriff, in Hunter's assessment, was determined to do nothing and was more concerned with his election for county treasurer, and Lester, in defiance of all common sense, refused to stop. Black told Hunter, "Lay down on that damn sheriff. Have him do his full duty. I cannot send troops until requested by the sheriff."[13]

Despite his certainty that violence was imminent, Hunter issued a statement to calm the public's nerves: "After our conference this morning I feel confident that the officials of the coal company and the local civil authorities arrived at an understanding which will preclude any troubles or disorder. I do not fear any trouble after the conference we had this morning." Hunter very disingenuously also stated that the sheriff was "thoroughly competent to handle any emergency. We have every confidence in their performing every official duty."

Despite his proclaimed confidence, Hunter immediately requested Thaxton to swear in more deputies. The sheriff refused and told Hunter he had enough deputies and that troops were not needed. Outside of the courthouse, more miners had gathered, some of them carrying weapons.

Not content to stand by as the tension mounted, Hunter made another trip to the mine this time accompanied by Thaxton, State Senator William Sneed, president of the UMWA district and a Shriner, and reporters for the local newspapers. In front of witnesses, McDowell openly offered Hunter a bribe of $50 a day if he would bring troops to protect them, an offer Hunter promptly refused. Hunter observed a stockpile of weapons and about 75,000 rounds of ammunition. On return to Marion, Hunter again pleaded with Thaxton to take action and told him that the troops were ready when he requested them.

In the Lewis-Farrington fight within the union, Local President William Sneed, who had first starting working in a mine at age 14, and Vice President Fox Hughes were Lewis allies, while Board Member Hugh Willis, who earned a reputation as a peacemaker for preventing a labor dispute with the Coal Belt interurban rail line before the vital link was shut, was in the Farrington camp. Sometime later that same day, Sneed sent a telegram to John L. Lewis asking him if the Steam Shovel Men's Union was sanctioned by the AFL to work the mine as Lester claimed. "If

4. Detonators

agreement exists have authorities stop their men scabbing on union coal miners at once." Lewis was attending an AFL convention in Cincinnati, answering charges that he was responsible for the imprisonment of Alex Howat, when he received Sneed's telegram. The following morning Sneed received a reply:

> Indianapolis, Ind., June 19, 1922
> William J. Sneed
> Pres. Sub-District 10
> District 12, U.M.W. of A.
> Herrin, Illinois
>
> Your wire of eighteenth. Steam Shovel Men's Union was suspended from affiliation with American Federation of Labor some years ago. It was also ordered suspended from the mining department of the American Federation of Labor at the Atlantic City convention. We now find that this outlaw organization is permitting its members to act as strike breakers at numerous strip pits in Ohio. This organization is furnishing steam shovel engineers to work under armed guards with strike breakers. It is not true that any form of arrangement exists by and between this organization and the mining department or any other branch of the American Federation of Labor permitting them to work under such circumstances. We have, through representative, officially taken this question up with the officers of the Steam Shovel Men's Union and have failed to secure any satisfaction. Representatives of our organization are justified in treating this crowd as an outlaw organization and in viewing its members in the same light as do any other common strike breakers.
>
> (Signed) John L. Lewis[14]

Lewis' telegram was read and repeated on the streets of Marion and Herrin. Both telegrams were printed in full by the *Marion Daily Republican* the same day, and by other local newspapers in later editions. The phrases "outlaw organization" and "common strike breakers" rung in the streets. About 600 union supporters, which by now included miners from other Illinois counties and, by some reports, miners from as far away as Kentucky, held an open-air meeting in the Herrin cemetery south of town. What was said at this meeting is unknown, other than the fact that the Lewis telegram was read again. In light of subsequent events, those in attendance kept quiet. Presumably, one of those in attendance was a local farmer and part-time miner, President of UMWA Local 655 Otis Clark, whose anger was already boiling to the edge of violence. Thaxton was informed of the gathering but characteristically did nothing.

Around this time, Lester boarded a north bound train for Chicago. Later that day Otis Alexander, a night watchman at the nearby Watson mine that shared a telephone party line with the Lester mine—a common arrangement in the first half of the 20th century—listened in on a conversations between Lester and McDowell. Alexander said Lester told McDowell that hundreds of union supporters were converging on Herrin from nearby mining communities. "Let them come," Alexander heard McDowell tell Lester, "I don't think they will all get here."

5

First Blood

Wednesday, June 21, was the first day of summer and the longest day of the year. In Cincinnati William Green, the secretary-treasurer of the UMWA, told the press the miners were determined "to fight it out if it takes all summer" echoing the words of a Civil War general.[1] Green's definition of fight was to continue the strike with the hope that "reason, sense and good judgment" would bring the coal operators to the table to hammer out a new contract. "Along with the suffering of the miners must inevitably come great inconvenience to the public and perhaps suffering as well. If this coal strike is to continue, the supply will be wholly inadequate to meet public requirements when fall and winter comes." But in Herrin that day the definition of fight was taking on a different meaning.

Col. Hunter began his day calling on the sheriff's office. Everything was fine, a deputy told him. There was no trouble overnight and there was no need for additional deputies.

Hunter found Thaxton in Duty's office, where he repealed his appeal only to receive the same answer. With mounting apprehension, Hunter sought out C.R. Erdington, Secretary of the Greater Marion Association, and asked him to form a citizens' committee to deal with the crisis. Erdington agreed and sent local businessman Charles Hamilton to the Lester mine to ask McDowell to resign. Outside of the property, as the strikebreakers were loading the last of the 70 rail cars of coal they shipped from the mine, a crowd was seen gathering. Hamilton returned and suggested the committee contact Lester directly. At about 9:15 a.m. they found him at the Great Northern Hotel in Chicago. Lester, perhaps now realizing the danger which had motivated his sudden escape from Herrin to the safety of Chicago, caved and agreed to shut down the mine. Lester asked Hamilton to pass the word to McDowell. McDowell, seeing the mob forming over the top of the mounds, agreed.

Unknown to the citizens' committee, while they were negotiating a settlement with Lester and McDowell, the situation grew much worse. That morning ten more strikebreakers arrived from Chicago at the train station in Carbondale. They were met at the station by a Dodge truck and a car from the Lester mine. They climbed in the back of the truck and set off east for the mine. The small convoy passed over the Fozrad Bridge, spanning the Big Muddy River near the border between Jackson and Williamson counties. A car in front of them slowed and began firing (by some accounts, the car sped up and fired shots into the air). As if receiving a signal, gunfire erupted from both sides of the road. The truck and car were riddled with bullets. The truck driver, Sidney Morrison of Chicago, was hit in the spine. Three others were less seriously wounded. Several strikebreakers dove into the river and fled into the countryside. George Drew, whose farm was near the bridge, later said he heard about 75 gunshots. A half hour later, two wounded men approached his house asking for help. They took him to the scene of the ambush and found Morrison. Drew took all of them to the hospital in Carbondale.

First reports of the ambush by strikebreakers were unclear whether it had happened in Jackson or Williamson County. Sheriff Thaxton, accompanied by Duty, left to investigate, and found the truck and the wounded already in Carbondale. Sidney Morrison was taken back to Chicago and died of his wounds a short time later. Thaxton spoke to W.J. Brown, the clerk of the municipal court in Carbondale. "The Sam T. Brush riots wouldn't be one, two or three with what is going to happen in the next few hours," Thaxton told Brown, although he later denied ever saying it.

Perhaps word of the ambush reached the crowds gathering on the streets of Herrin and Marion, or perhaps things had reached a critical mass on their own. Whether or not they knew of the armed attack, crowds flooded into every hardware store in both towns and began looting them for rifles, shotguns, handguns, and ammunition. The store owners were powerless against the flood of angry, cursing men grabbing the weapons. "Charge it to the union," one yelled as he left with a rifle.[2] In the Herrin Supply Company, manager Charles Shaffauer confronted several men wanting to take guns and ammunition without paying for them. "We want to know whether you will let us have these guns and ammunition. The Local is good for it." Someone called Hugh Willis and handed the phone to Shaffauer. "Charlie, there's some of the boys want to get some ammunition to shoot some birds. You let them have it and just make a duplicate of the tickets and bring them to me." The men left the store with twelve rifles, six revolvers and ammunition.

5. First Blood

By now the crowd was openly talking of attacking the Lester mine. In Marion, the American Legion post took their firearms to the police station for safekeeping. Their fears were well founded, as a group later appeared at the post demanding the guns. The hardware stores were soon cleared of firearms. Neither the sheriff's deputies nor local police were seen. Miners in West Frankfort also raided the hardware stores and supporters around the region gathered their personal rifles and shotguns and began leaving for Herrin. One unverified report said a convoy of fifty automobiles left Marion.

It was now noon. Some of the armed men seemed to organize themselves in the Herrin cemetery. Some, without leaders or an apparent plan, began marching toward the mine. Cars bearing license plates from Indiana, Kentucky and other states were parked everywhere on the streets along with strange cars from other parts of Illinois.

In the place called Crenshaw Crossing, a clump of houses along the road, almost within sight of the mine, the crowd of around 600 men began preparing for battle. Grover Keely, a union miner, at the scene saw five strikebreakers escorted by an armed band. The five had tried to escape to the Herrin train station. The prisoners said McDowell had told them if anyone tried to leave the guards would kill them. One of them said "We don't want any trouble, but will go to McDowell and try to get him to stop work."[3] Two of the five volunteered to approach McDowell and turned back in the direction of the mine. At that moment, approximately three o'clock, shots were fired from the mine. The engineer in the locomotive blew the train's shrieking whistle. McDowell was in the office talking to Fred Bernard, one of the contract commissary cooks, about obtaining food and ice when the shooting began. Bernard and the other food service workers climbed into a rail car where they hid throughout the night. Later in the day Keely escorted the two unharmed prisoners to the Marion train station.

Several hundred miners were closing in on the mine. The machine gun opened fire on them, along with the high-powered rifles. McDowell and mine timekeeper Allen Findley stood on the edge of the mine. McDowell looked into the woods and pointed at a dark shape. "Is that a man?" McDowell asked Findley. Findley said no but McDowell fired, striking the figure, his arms flying upward as he fell down. The bloody body of 45-year-old Jordy (sometimes spelled Gerodie) Henderson, a local miner, was discovered about half a mile distance from the mine. His friends carried his body back through the crowds at Crenshaw Crossing on their way

The Herrin Massacre of 1922

to Herrin. A Lithuanian miner, 22-year-old Joe Petkewicz (sometimes identified as Petkeuicius, Pitchovie, or Pitchonis), nicknamed "Pitch Cabbage," was wounded on the field and died in a few hours. At least two other wounded were taken to the Herrin hospital. Henderson was well known locally, and the news of his death spread rapidly. A story circulated that McDowell had personally killed Henderson while perched in a makeshift sniper's nest in the elevated bucket of the steam shovel. Apropos of nothing, it was McDowell's 28th birthday

The miners, some of whom had served in the war, surrounded the mine and returned fire. One person in the mob was Army veteran Otis Clark, a 45-year-old miner and local union official described as being of medium height with brown hair and grey eyes. Among his other duties, Clark had signed the paperwork for the death benefits of miners and their families. In the union infighting, Clark was a supporter of Alex Howart.

None of this gun fire was immediately known in Marion, just a few miles away. At 3:10 p.m., McDowell phoned Hunter in a panic to tell him the mine was under attack and that about 500 shots had been fired. Hunter hung up and tried to reach Thaxton, but the sheriff was still in Carbondale. Hunter ordered Deputy Storm to gather every available person and stop the fighting in Herrin. Storm replied he could handle it without the sheriff. McDowell called again a few minutes later and reported that situation was growing worse, and again asked Hunter to bring in the troops. In another 15 minutes, Assistant Superintendent John Shoemaker, William Lester's brother-in-law, told Hunter that one of his men had been shot. McDowell grabbed the telephone out of his hand and again pleaded for troops.

Earlier in the day, Lester had called Gen. Black to request troops. Black had called Hunter who told him that at that moment a truce had been arranged and that there was no trouble. As a precaution, Black ordered Illinois National Guard units in Mt. Vernon, Cairo and Salem—all in southern Illinois—to standby and be ready if called. After the news of ambush and the gunfight, Hunter updated Black, who still was waiting for Thaxton to make the formal request for assistance.

By now Thaxton and Duty had returned from Carbondale. Duty wanted to go to Herrin immediately, but Thaxton advised waiting until the following morning. At approximately 4:30, Hunter called McDowell to suggest a cease fire, to which the frightened man who had bragged of his toughness immediately agreed. Hunter called UMWA Local Vice President Fox Hughes, who also agreed to a truce. Hunter arranged that each side would display a white flag. The strikebreakers would be allowed

5. First Blood

to leave unharmed and the mine would shut down. McDowell ordered a white flag raised on the side of the mine facing Crenshaw Crossing. As a strikebreaker raised a bedsheet over the ridge, he was fired at about fifty times but was not hit. Hughes stuffed a piece of white muslin cloth into his shirt and drove to the battlefield.

At Crenshaw Crossing, hundreds of armed men moved on the roads. A representative of the Axton-Fisher Tobacco Company was handing out free samples of Old Hill Side pipe tobacco, Booster Twist and White Mule Twist plug tobacco, and White Clown cigarettes to the crowd. Hughes later claimed that he could not see the white flag that should have been hoisted over the mine amid the heavy firing. The makeshift flag stayed inside his shirt as the bullets continued to fly and the fighting continued unabated. Many of those inside the mine hired as equipment operators picked up a rifle and joined the guards on the line of battle. They had little choice, as McDowell had told them the guards would shoot anyone who tried to leave and that they were as safe inside of the mine as outside.

Around dusk, a solitary biplane flew over the mine dropping homemade dynamite bombs. The guards fired wildly at the plane but apparently missed it, their fire as ineffective as the bombardment itself. Shots were fired from the airplane, hitting nothing but the bare ground throwing up dust. After a second pass over the mine, the airplane flew away. No one at the time determined the identity of the pilot or where the airplane came from, and with the distance of time it will never be known. It was not the first aerial bombing in anger of America, the tactic having been just as ineffective in the Battle of Blair Mountain the year before. (The same tactic was repeated in Williamson County a few years later, when a gang dropped bombs on a rival's headquarters.)

The miners on the ground made better use of dynamite. The explosive was easy to obtain legally or to steal from local mines that used tons of the material. Many miners were skilled and experienced in using it every working day. The miner army targeted the railroad spur cut into the man-made slopes and blew it up. They also destroyed the dam, flooding the excavations below, and the power lines leading into the mine property. One of the steam shovels was damaged. The sounds of explosions thundered through the countryside and were heard and felt as far away as Marion, spreading a growing fear among the residents.

Darkness began to fall. The gunfire from both sides dwindled. The strikebreakers and the guards huddled down in makeshift shelters under railroad cars with wooden ties piled up in makeshift forts. In Herrin, the streets teemed with roaming bands of men, some on foot, some driving up and down the streets. Music from pianos and Victrolas scratching out the latest tunes spread from the open windows into the streets. After an evening of watching silent movies, theatergoers in Herrin and Marion found large loud mobs roaming the streets. In the restless throngs, rumors spread like a virus. More than two union brothers were killed, some said. How many? Someone heard someone else said they saw ten dead men. Or was it more like twelve? Doubtless a number of the crowd had made the very easy discovery of Herrin and Marion's bootleggers and speakeasies

A band of about 50 armed men heard that Lester was hiding in a house on East Thorn Street. Finding no one there the mob left the house untouched. Another group twisted the news that some weeks before mine owner A.B. McLaren had expressed interest in bringing a steam shovel to his operation, like the ones at the Lester mine, as part of a false rumor that he intended to break the strike like Lester. They searched for him until they were satisfied that McLaren had no such intentions.

In Marion, State's Attorney Duty called another conference. Hugh Willis, Col. Hunter, Major Davis, Sheriff Thaxton, Judge D.T. Hartwell and a handful of others planned their next move. The consensus was that Thaxton go immediately to the mine with enough deputies to enforce the truce. The sheriff refused to go there at night but agreed to go at first light around six a.m. Hunter updated Black, telling him that the truce would be enforced.

Otis Alexander, again eavesdropping on the party line, heard Lester, who had supposedly agreed to the truce, tell McDowell to "raise the white flag and get some union men into the mine and hold them: Make some kind of agreement and then rearrange your guard."[4]

Hugh Willis left the conference and drove to Herrin. Standing before the union hall he addressed the crowd gathered there. "We have the mine well-guarded and surrounded so no one can get out and there will be nothing more doing until morning when we can see," Willis said. "What I have been most interested in is prevailing on the sheriff not to get troops down here before we can get possession of the fellows. The sheriff has been very loyal to our cause and we must not forget him this fall when election time comes. They should have more sense than to come down here but as long as they did, damn them, let them take what they get."

Midnight passed. It was now June 22, 1922.

6

Stop the Breed of Them

During the night there was scattered gunfire and explosions. The strikebreakers huddled under the heavy equipment and railroad cars, surrounded by the armed miners, cut off from the outside world. One strikebreaker later remembered hearing sounds of military drilling among the miners. The power lines had been cut and their only connection, a party line telephone, promised no relief. They had stockpiles of weapons and ammunition, some food and water stored in the commissary car, but little hope of outside aid. Some peered over the mounds of earth, reaching a height of sixty feet to look into the darkness, broken by scattered farm lights, and car headlights moving between them and the faint glow on of the distant towns. There was enough light for some to see the white sheet still hanging from the pole rising above the crest of the mounds. A few, the exact number can never be known, may have looked into the darkness and risked death by escaping from the mine, moving into the unfamiliar countryside, struggling to find a way out through the armed miners and a hostile population, risking a secret death and burial in an unmarked grave. Perhaps one or more of them escaped into the night and made it to safety.[1] No one knows what happened to them and no one at the time, strikebreaker or miner, ever said anything about those who escaped, never to be heard from again. Most of the strikebreakers huddled under steel railroad cars, inches away from men they scarcely knew, some holding weapons they had not been hired to carry and wondering how they ever ended up here in danger in a distant country.

Robert Officer, the mine's bookkeeper and a graduate of the University of Pennsylvania, had talked to Col. Hunter during the previous day's fighting.[2] Lester, Hunter had assured him, had authorized the surrender of the mine. The bookkeeper, suddenly a long way from the Ivy League, was issued a rifle which he carried with him during the night. As dawn broke, those left inside of the mine had little hope of escape or rescue.

The Herrin Massacre of 1922

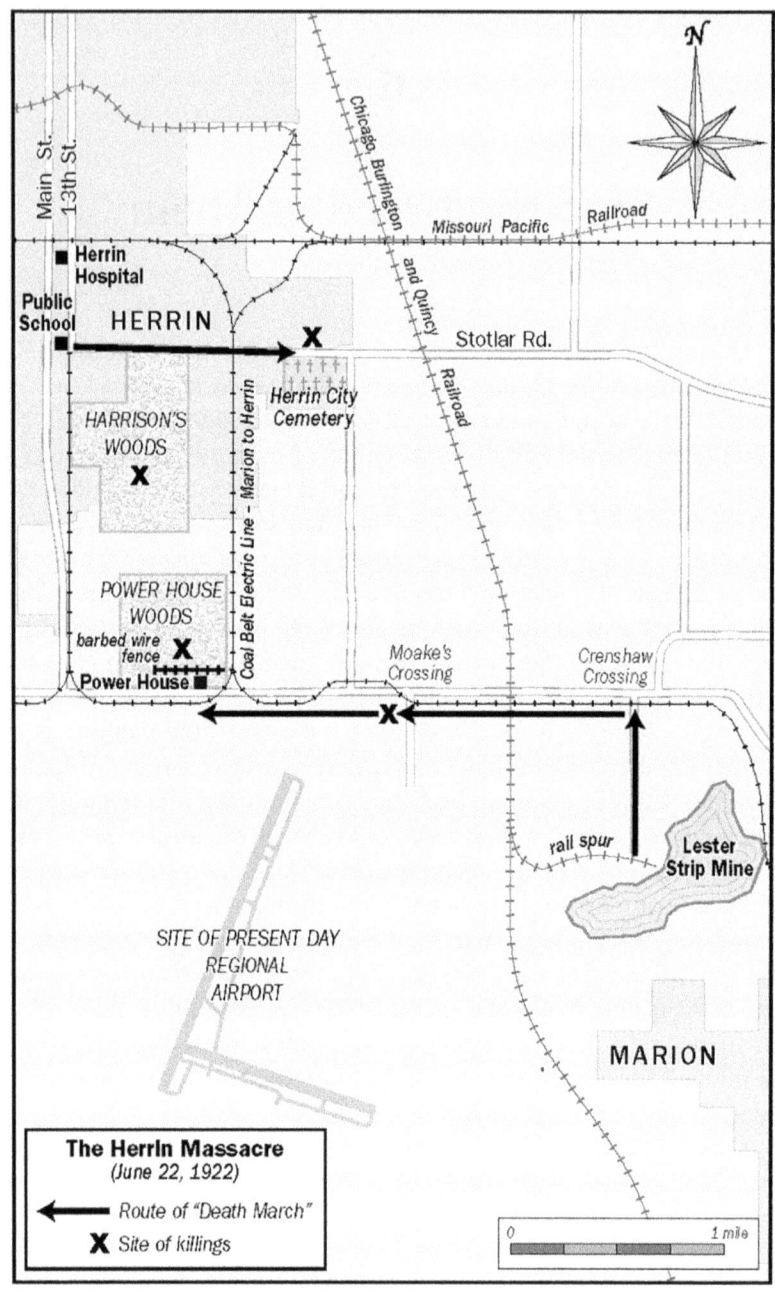

Map of area of the Herrin Massacre.

6. Stop the Breed of Them

Some parts of the mine were already occupied by the attacking miners. The tense silence was punctuated by the occasional shattering explosions destroying the heavy equipment. The telephone line was still open in the morning, but C.K. McDowell could not find help at the other end. No troops were coming to stop the assault. Robert Officer was trapped along with the other strikebreakers and guards. Perhaps as an act of defiance or a surrender to futility, someone took down the white flag. Waiters from the commissary car brought pots of coffee to the crouching, tense men.

During the night, the attacking miners, some of whom had recently served in the military in the Great War, had moved their positions closer to the mine.[3] The two sides were close enough to communicate, and around first light informal, shouted negotiations began. Bernard Jones tied an apron taken from the commissary car to a broomstick and raised the white flag again.[4] Carrying the flag, Jones approached the miners. "I want to talk to your leader," he said.

An armed man stood up. "What do you want?"

Jones said he and the others wanted to surrender if they had safe passage. "Come on out and we'll get you out of the county," the miner said.

Word of the surrender quickly spread. About three hundred miners, still holding their rifles and handguns, entered the mine through the railroad spar and approached the strikebreakers. The disarmed men stood waiting with their hands over their heads, some smiling with relief that the seizure was over and volunteering that they did not know what they were getting into when they were hired to come to Herrin. Some of the miners and strikebreakers shook hands with each other. Some of the miners fired their guns in the air and a few fired into the ground near the line of prisoners. Others of the victorious miners, cheering loudly, descended upon the scabs and began striking them with their rifle butts and pistol handles, as well as kicking them. Some began looting the commissary rail car and others began wiring dynamite to the steam shovels and machinery. A few others went directly to the office and its safe. They were later seen in town waving around a wad of bills.

The surrendered strikebreakers were powerless in the face of the mob, some of whom wanted to take revenge. No one person was in charge in the chaos but someone in the crowd ordered the prisoners lined up by twos for the march to the railroad. McDowell, the boss to the last, also ordered his men to form a line. Some of the strikebreakers tried to leave with suitcases, which the miners stripped from them, dumping the contents on the ground, saying "You won't need that where you're going." Others in the crowd ordered the prisoners to remove their shoes.

C. K. McDowell was thrown into the front of the line of prisoners. He was singled out for abuse, both physical and verbal, as the mass of excited miners and strikebreakers began to move northward to the railroad. About the same time the strikebreakers surrendered and began their march, Col. Hunter was waiting outside the sheriff's office in Marion as agreed. He remained alone waiting for Thaxton whose whereabouts were unknown. The one place it was certain he could not be found was the mine. In fact, not a single deputy or other law enforcement officer was at the mine as the crowd moved out.

As the mass of men began moving northward, the number of armed miners increased with new men appearing from all directions joining the contingent that had entered the mine, and agreed to safely escort the prisoners. Many of those without guns carried pitchforks, razors, rocks, butcher knives and clubs. The stench of moonshine from the growing mob became stronger, and some of the strikebreakers noticed the bloodshot eyes of some of their captors. Locals lined both sides of the impromptu march to watch and taunt the prisoners. Miner Phillip Fontanetta pointed to prisoner Otis Lawrence and asked a woman if she would like a lock of Lawrence's hair after he killed him. The woman declined the offer. Fontanetta pointed his revolver at Lawrence's head and said, "I think I'll shoot it out anyway."

"Don't do it. You'll shoot one of our men," another said.

Further along the way, James Brown, an African American wearing an old army helmet and carrying an antique flint lock rifle, joined the march. "The articles of war state that after a prisoner has been captured, he shall be given good treatment," witnesses heard Brown say.[5] "I've been in the war. These men are prisoners. Tain't right." Despite his words Brown struck some of the prisoners with his helmet.

As the crowd grew, the anger and hostility grew. McDowell, leading the line of prisoners, was the focal point of the rage. His swaggering arrogance and violent threats were thrown back in his face. The rumor that he had personally shot the two dead miners less than eighteen hours earlier, along with his reputation for breaking unions, fueled the hatred. Painfully limping, bleeding, dragging his artificial leg along the road, the exhausted and terrified McDowell struggled to keep up as the crowd grew more agitated.

"They're nothing but strikebreakers and we ought to kill them all,"

6. Stop the Breed of Them

someone shouted. Someone struck McDowell on the head with a revolver, nearly felling him, and another smashed a rifle into the small of his back to push him on. "There's no use going on with him," another in the crowd said.

The mob and the line of prisoners reached Crenshaw Crossing, about one mile from the mine. The march stopped. There was a small store at the crossing with a telephone where someone in the mob made a call, presumably to the local union office. The unknown miner who had promised the prisoners safe passage tried to address the crowd, but it was apparent he was no longer in charge. He was not heard from again, according to surviving strikebreakers.

Standing on the front steps of the store, holding a rifle over his head, Otis Clark shouted, "I have been in this fight for five days and I believe in starting at the head to stop a proposition. I believe in taking them, everyone, out, kill them and stopping the breed of them."

"I can't walk any farther. If you are going to kill me, do it now and don't let me suffer any longer," McDowell said, as blood streamed down his face into his blinking eyes. Otis Clark and another local, Oscar Howard, approached McDowell and struck him in the ribs and on the forehead, knocking him to the ground. The two picked up McDowell and dragged him a short distance.

"You Goddamned son of a bitch, you," Clark shouted. "I'm going to kill you and tear you to pieces and use you for bait to catch the rest of the scabs with. You put Alexander Howat in jail, and I am going to send your soul to hell."

Out of sight of most of the mob, at least three shots rang out. In a nearby farmhouse a mother ordered her children to stand inside a stone fireplace to protect them from the gunfire outside. Clark and Howard came back shouting that they had killed Old Peg Leg. Most of the crowd roared approval but a few tried to calm the mob. Some later said they thought McDowell's death would satisfy the crowd's rage, and for a moment it seemed that it did. But the calls to kill all of the strikebreakers grew louder.

The mass of prisoners and the surrounding miners turned west down the road towards a spot known as Moakes Crossing. More armed men joined the crowd along with women, among them Clark's wife Lizzie, urging the miners to kill the prisoners. About five minutes later as the crowd moved away a few people came out of their nearby homes and found McDowell's bullet ridden body lying on the ground.

The Herrin Massacre of 1922

At Moakes Crossing, the miners who had negotiated the safe conduct of prisoners were clearly no longer in control. The dynamic of the mob had shifted, taking on a life beyond the individuals shouting and waving weapons at the helpless captives. Some of the miners addressed a black man, possibly James Brown. "See these white sons of bitches that we don't think as much of we do you, colored boy?"[6]

Near Moakes Crossing was a power plant for the interurban trolley line. Just beyond the building was a clump of woods of oaks and blueberry bushes. A four-strand barbed wire fence, about chest high, ran through the trees. As the growing mass of people continued to move near Moakes Crossing, UMWA Local President Hugh Willis arrived in his car. Willis talked to Clark and several others. "Listen, don't go killing these folks on a public highway. There are too many women and children around to do that. Take them over in the woods and give it to them. Kill all you can," Willis said. Willis drove away and Clark ordered the prisoners moved into the woods. As they herded them towards the fence at gunpoint, someone shouted, "Only those with guns can enter the woods."

No one on either side could have any illusions about what would happen next. McDowell's murder was less than fifteen minutes ago, and the prisoners certainly knew they would be killed. The miners leading them

The barbed wire fence where the killing began (Williamson County Historical Society).

6. Stop the Breed of Them

into the woods knew they were about to commit murder. No one knows precisely how many entered the woods but there were at least 45 prisoners and perhaps 300 miners. They were roughly lined up in front of the fence as the gunmen took positions in a disorganized approximation of a military firing squad. The gun men cocked their rifles and handguns. "We are going to give you a chance for your lives," one of the miners said. Immediately the first shots were fired into the already moving line of prisoners trying to escape.

The sounds of gunfire were mixed with screams of pain and panic. Some fell dead after the first volley. Some who were wounded fell, while some wounded scrambled through or over the fence, tearing their clothing and flesh on the strands of barbed wire. Others who were not shot ran for their lives.

Several men wounded by the first shots became entangled in the barbed wire. The miners advanced, firing additional shots directly into them. One of the wounded saw another injured man caught upright in the fence as he was struck repeatedly with bullets. "You son of a bitch, I can make you fall," a gunman screamed as he blew the man's brains out with a point-blank shot.

The dead and wounded lay together near the fence. As waves of gunmen moved pass them some, stopped to check if those on the ground were dead. William Cairns was caught in the fence, bleeding from two gunshots, when he saw another strikebreaker against a tree as the miners beat him. "You big son of a bitch, we can kill you," miner Peter Hiller yelled as he fired his gun.

As Cairns lay wounded, he saw others around him. "Goodbye Jack," one of them said to no one, "I am coming." Then the man died.

John Shoemaker, Lester's brother-in-law, was wounded and made it over the fence before losing consciousness. Sherman Holman, the mine guard, who two days earlier had gloated to his ex-wife about how tough he was, tripped over Shoemaker's body as he ran from the fence. Holman's head rested on Shoemaker's arm as a gunman came up to Shoemaker and kicked his body. "This son of a bitch is still breathing. Anybody got a shell?"[7] Phillip Fontanetta walked up and, as Holman watched, fired point blank into Shoemaker's face. Holman remained still as the blast of dust and blood hit him.

Another wounded strikebreaker, Edward Rose, played dead as the gunmen closed in on him. "By God, some of them are still breathing. They're hard to kill, ain't they?"[8] Rose braced himself as the man fired into his back. Rose did not flinch, and the mob moved on to others, firing into the fallen men, dead or alive.

While the murders continued in the woods, two strikebreakers had better luck. Fred Bernard's cap was shot off his head before he reached some brush near the fence as others fled past him. Bernard found mine guard Whitey Williams hiding in ground cover. The miners soon discovered the pair. They struck Williams, who began crying and praying. Bernard told the miners he was just a cook and that Williams was a waiter. Bernard asked the gunmen if any of them belonged to the Knights of Pythias or the Elks, as he did. He gave the club sign to one of the men who summoned other lodge members over to the pair. They agreed to help them escape in a car but then decided the safest course was to walk out while acting as unconcerned as possible. The lodge brothers escorted Bernard and Williams to Carbondale, where they caught a train for Chicago.

Those who were not killed or wounded near the fence ran on for the lives, the gunmen in pursuit, howling like wolves. George Harrison, who worked a farm north of the power plant on the outskirts of Herrin, saw a group of about twenty-five men chasing a man across his corn field into the woods. He saw some of the pursuers fire at the fleeing man, the dust flying behind them as they ran. He and his son Fred, home for the summer from the University of Illinois, entered the woods and encountered several local men they knew. They saw another group of miners with two prisoners. The father and son left the scene. From the safety of the barn, the Harrisons heard shots. About three hours later they ventured into the woods again. There they discovered three bodies on the ground and the man they saw running across their field hanging from a tree. The hanged man was riddled with multiple gunshot wounds, apparently used for target practice. The following day they discovered a fifth body on their farm.

Harold Graves was hoeing strawberries with his mother on the family farm when they saw a man being chased by a mob who was firing on him.[9] The mother and son ran through a cornfield, falling down along the way in a panic. When they reached the house, the yard was filled with angry, armed men. In the afternoon on their way to the mailbox Harold and his seven-year-old brother Allen discovered two men hiding under some bushes. One was already dead and the other had a broken leg. Their father called the Storme funeral home. Allen led the ambulance crew to the them, and they took the injured man to the hospital. Years later, Harold, looking back on his childhood, would remember the armed mob in

6. Stop the Breed of Them

his front yard as "otherwise good men now ruled by the lowest common denominator, hatred for those scabs."

Patrick O'Rourke, one of the mine guards brought down from Chicago, was shot twice after he made it over the fence. He hid in the brush as the gunman swept past him.

After it seemed clear, he set off toward Herrin hoping to escape. He cautiously walked close to a road, carefully watching. A car came down the road and sensing danger O'Rourke ran to a cellar at a nearby house. A woman, her identity lost to history, tried to convince the miners that O'Rourke was not there, but he had been spotted by the men in the car. Despite the Good Samaritan's pleas, they took him into custody and began pistol whipping him on the head.

One of his captors wanted to shoot him immediately, another wanted to lynch him with a rope. The men robbed O'Rourke of his wallet and shoes. After some discussion O'Rourke was thrown into the car. As it was later reported, along the sides of the road were caps and blood covered shirts, marking the route of the fleeing strikebreakers. They drove into Herrin to a schoolhouse and took him inside. O'Rourke found five other men from the mine being held prisoner, among them Howard Hoffman.

About the same time the six men were held in the schoolhouse Associated Press reporter Don Ewing arrived in Marion from Chicago. News of the previous day's warfare had already reached the outside world and Ewing was only the first of many journalists making the trip to Williamson County. In Marion, Ewing hired a taxi to take him to the Lester Mine. When he arrived around 9:30, the strikebreakers had already been taken away. The mine was on fire and about a hundred men, women and children as young as ten were swarming over the compound in a carnival celebration. The locals told Ewing that some of the strikebreakers had already been killed. Ewing returned to his hired car and told the driver to head for Herrin.

In Herrin, the fate of the six men had been decided. O'Rourke, Hoffman and the others were roped around the neck and led out in the streets of Herrin. Lining both sides of the street were hundreds of spectators, cursing, threatening, screaming hatred and abuse. The six barefoot, exhausted and bloodied men were forced to crawl down the center of the street, their sweat and blood mixing with dirt. One tried to hold in the blood from a wound near his waist. Another held his blood covered forearm with his good arm. Leva Mann demanded he swing his arms. When he did not, Mann struck him. Herding them like cattle to

The Herrin Massacre of 1922

the slaughterhouse, the miners, led by Leva Mann, dragged them along with the ropes, proudly displaying their captives. "God damn you, if you never prayed before you had better do it now," someone in the crowd shouted. "Nearer my God to thee," another mockingly called out. The six were allowed to stand and they staggered, panting, terrified and in agony as they passed the well-stocked storefronts, the latest model automobiles, the facades of respectable establishments and the foundations of family pride in the "liveliest place in Southern Illinois." Herrin had revealed its true face for the world to see.

The six men were led about a mile to the Herrin City Cemetery and the growing crowd followed. "Let's make soap of them," someone shouted. Exactly how many were in the crowd that morning can never be known, but it was at least a thousand and some placed it as high as 3,000. In any event, it was a large and very supportive crowd, standing amid the tombstones, standing on top of graves, about to witness the final act of the massacre.

As the crowd gathered in the cemetery for a better view, the six prisoners were roped together around the neck. O'Rourke was shot in the ankle and as he fell, he pulled the other five down with him. As he lay on the ground, someone shot him in the shoulder and the arm. A gunman shot each of the six helpless men at close range. The crowd stood watching as they bled on the ground, the life slowly draining out of them. A few women in the crowd with cameras were confronted and their cameras were destroyed. Joe Carnhagi began shooting at random. He reloaded and hit one of the six. He then fired into Howard Hoffman's shoulder. A local doctor, O.F. Shipman, saw the blood spurt out a foot high. At about this time, Don Ewing and his driver reached the cemetery. The road was congested with parked cars, so Ewing got out and walked the rest of the way. He saw the six on the ground. Ewing checked on the men, finding three of them apparently dead or nearly dead. O'Rourke, Hoffman and another were barely alive. O'Rourke looked at Ewing and asked for some water. Ewing ran to a nearby house with a pump in the yard and filled a bucket. He was blocked by armed miner Bert Grace. A woman carrying a baby in her arms screamed at O'Rourke, "I'll see you in hell before you get any water." Grace then approached Hoffman. He placed his boot on one of Hoffman's open wounds and put his weight on it. Ewing was powerless to do anything as the spectacle continued. O'Rourke called out the name and address of his mother and asked someone to notify her of his death, much to the amusement of the crowd. After

6. Stop the Breed of Them

about a half an hour, someone pulled a knife out of his pocket and slowly and deliberately slashed the throats of each of the six men. O'Rourke passed out. As the bodies lay before the crowd, someone stepped forward and urinated on them.

Ewing left the cemetery and found a telephone in Herrin. He called the St. Louis AP office and dictated the news to the world. The show over, and with the news that the Sheriff was finally on his way, the crowd left the cemetery. Sheriff Thaxton was in fact on his way. After making Col. Hunter wait outside his office, Thaxton and Hunter went to the mine after the mob had left. Thinking, or wishing to believe, that everything had gone well they returned to Marion. There they learned of the killings and drove to Moakes Crossing. Thaxton found the dead and wounded near the fence. He ordered the wounded taken to the Herrin City Hospital. There, under the direction of Dr. J.T. Black, the wounded were well treated. The doctor, a short man weighing about 110 pounds, was later asked if he was afraid for the staff or the patients. "If you had seen 50 to 100 men running around trying to find someone to kill, you would have perhaps thought we were in danger." Among the wounded were Sherman Holman, William Cairns, Edward Rose, who was left paralyzed from the waist down by the point blank shot to his back, and Ignace Kubinis, whose leg was so shattered by a sawed-off shotgun blast that it had to be amputated at the hip.

At the cemetery Thaxton and his deputies found four dead and O'Rourke and Hoffman barely alive. Hoffman died the next day in the hospital. The dead were taken to the vacant Dillard Building in downtown Herrin.

Together the dead lay in rows, each of top of a box with a brick under its head, their bodies already stiffened with rigor mortis and marked by livid pools of settled, residual blood where they fell on the ground. Their open bullet wounds, slashed throats and other knife wounds, the darkening blood stains, the dirt and mud of the mine and of the chase, their lifeless staring eyes were on display for Herrin. Unshackled by the chains of political correctness, the Associated Press reporter witnessing the public display of the bodies wrote of "the dead of a half a dozen nationalities, with sloping foreheads of the Slav, the high profiles of the native born, the long mustaches of eastern Europe."

A steady stream of people filed unto the Dillard Building to look at the dead on display. Some spectators silently filed past the bodies, but most either mocked the dead or hurled insults at their bodies. Many brought their children to view the dead. A woman holding a toddler glared at the bodies. "Take a look at what your papa did, kid."

The Herrin Massacre of 1922

"Well, it served them right," another said.

"Look at the dirty bums who tried to take the bread out of your mouths."

Some spat on the bodies, disturbing and scattering the gathering flies. In the summer heat, the bodies began to fill the air with the stench of death and decay. The display continued all night and into the next day as most of the bodies, unknown and unidentified, went unclaimed.

7

Outrage

The next morning a woman asked Hugh Willis if they had really killed the strikebreakers. No, he said, we just scared them so bad those fellers committed suicide. In the coming days there would be little laughter about the massacre in the world outside of Williamson County.

The massacre happened in the morning, early enough to make the afternoon newspapers, which were more common than today. The *Marion Evening Post* printed several hundred extra copies reporting on the morning's massacre. The news hit the wire services which reached all over the nation and overseas. The front page of the *St. Louis Post-Dispatch* carried the Associated Press report and stories from its unnamed correspondent. The newspaper ran a highlighted story telling how Adj. Gen. Black first learned of the violence when the paper called him in Springfield at 11 a.m. The *Post-Dispatch* correspondent's report was confused on many parts of the story, claiming McDowell had been beaten to death "apparently with the butt of revolvers" and that most of the strikebreakers were Italians. The AP report detailed the massacre in stark, brutal facts that instantly made Herrin, Illinois, both famous and infamous. The news was also passed by word of mouth. In another part of the county one Mrs. Eubans, the mother-in-law of a local judge, when told about the massacre began dancing a jig and said the strikebreakers got what they deserved.[1]

By Friday morning, a tsunami of shock, outrage and condemnation spread across the newspapers of America and the world. But unlike a tsunami, the reaction did not recede. Almost immediately, leading newspapers sent reporters to Herrin and editorial writers reached new heights of anger. The *Hartford Times* condemned the "5,000 moonshine whiskey-crazed miners." "Is Herrin a Part of the United States?" asked the *Detroit Free Press*. The *Augusta Journal* of Maine advocated, "Herrin, Illinois, should be ostracized, cut off from all communication with the outside world and left to soak in the blood they have spilled until they arrive

The Herrin Massacre of 1922

at such consciousness as is necessary in a civilized citizen." The *Seattle Star* reported the news of the massacre with an exclamation mark in the headline but ran it under a bigger story of "White Women Chained by Oriental Captors," predicting of a coming war between Western and Eastern civilizations.

One theme was to compare the massacre to the worst atrocities of the war, still fresh in the public's mind. "Belgium can congratulate herself that it was only Germans and not Illinois coal miners," wrote the *New York Tribune*. The *Baltimore Sun* called the miners "unspeakable moral

Editorial cartoon from *St. Louis Post Dispatch*.

7. Outrage

Turks who took part in this incredibly savage outbreak." The *New York News* wrote, "no massacre by savages was ever more bloodthirsty than that done by the mob on the strikebreakers at the Illinois coal mine." The *Washington Herald* imagined that the deposed German Kaiser must be reading the news with a cynical smile on his face. "The Cheka [the original KGB] of the Bolsheviki has nothing to its shame any blacker than this vengeful assassination of workers by workers," wrote the *Chicago Evening Post*. "Nothing we have ever read of the Russian pogroms, of the Turkish massacres of Christians, nor of the midnight descents of the Red Indians on the settlements of the American pioneers surpasses this Illinois horror in unfeeling ferocity and gloating cruelty," stated the *Knoxville Sentinel*. One Great War veteran, Richland Battle of Okmulgee, Oklahoma, wrote the *Manufacturers' Record* that he " had rather take my chances in a frontal attack on a machine gun nest than to attempt to assert my right, as a free born American citizen, to accept legitimate employment in any union field that I desired and particularly in and around Herrin, Ill."[2]

Many newspapers, along with condemning the bloodshed, noted that the massacre was a setback for organized labor, perhaps permanently. The *St. Louis Globe-Democrat* called it "the most brutal and horrifying crime that has ever stained the garments of organized labor." The *Chicago News* called the violence "a lasting blot" upon unions.

"It would be difficult to estimate how gravely the miners have injured their cause by converting themselves from strikers into murderers and criminals," wrote the *Macon Telegraph* of Georgia. The strongly anti-union *Los Angeles Times* blamed Samuel Gompers and John L. Lewis as equally guilty.

The *New Republic* magazine, while condemning the violence, saw a note of hope for organized labor. "In place of the cowed and passive aspect of labor in the steel strikes, we now have the atrocious retaliation of Herrin," said the editorial. "[I]t may be said without danger of contradiction that labor is exhibiting a new spirit: it is at least no longer willing to take a licking lying down." The *Nation* recounted the facts but said neither the miners nor the strikebreakers were completely responsible: "It was a consequence of the bitter industrial struggle in America whose causes society has been powerless or unwilling to remove and whose violent methods it has been unable to moderate. Perhaps the same spirit which gives America an ugly preeminence in homicide and which has led to our lynchings has brought it to pass that industrial disputes should be red with murder."

The Herrin Massacre of 1922

The *Outlook*, a weekly magazine, called Herrin "a successful massacre." "That Southern Illinois mining town has become known as the place where murder pays. Turks or Kurds who torture to death defenseless Armenians in order to rule the surviving population with a rod of terror now can enjoy the flattery of successful imitation in America."

William P. Helm, Jr., called in the same issue for the government to take control of the coal industry "at the mouth of the mine." "If we freeze or starve, we may have the dying satisfaction of knowing that, like hanging, our death is brought about in a manner so entirely justified by present laws that no possible objection can lie against it."

"The terrible tragedy at Herrin serves a useful lesson to Americans by revealing horrors they can expect in greater number in the future if Americal does not completely shut its gates to the immigrate," proclaimed the *Minneapolis Journal*. The *Chicago Journal* openly called for the execution of the miners. "Illinois means social disease," wrote the *Rochester Times* of New York. "Home of Lincoln Threatened with Disgrace," proclaimed the Illinois Manufacturers' Association, in a statement calling for a declaration of martial law and repeal of laws favoring unions. "Action on the part of the people is imperative. Are we to be cowards in the face of this barbarous massacre and astonishing defiance of law?"

The *Boston Herald* assigned blame on neither the operator nor the miners, but on Harding. "The President is on trial," the newspaper wrote. "Will he prove to the people of the United States that this is a free country; that any man has a right to work without getting the consent of a labor organization? Will he show that the owner of property has a right to operate his property without the consent of a labor organization? ... Will he in clear and forceful language notify the people of the United States that murder and violence must cease in labor disputes; that this is not a Soviet government?"

In a lengthy letter to the editor of the *New York Times* dated July 26, Millard Patterson of El Paso, Texas, analyzed the cause of the massacre and other labor unrest as "semi-Bolshevism," an attempt of workers to control the use of property without actually owning it. "The trouble in Herrin, Ill., and in the coal mining States generally," he wrote, "has grown out of the fact that men who have cared more for office or party than for either God or Government have not been willing to stand up for the fundamental law, and see that a company or an individual owning property shall be protected in the right to use it under the law, if it should take the whole power of the State to secure such protection."

7. Outrage

The foreign language press in America, particularly those serving the large mining communities, had divided views. The Croatian language *Hrvatski List*, published in New York, said the violence was counterproductive to the miners' interests. *Il Popolo*, an Italian daily, blamed the operators who refused to settle, as did the Russian *Russy Golos* and the *Novoye Russkoye Nepszava*. The trade journal *Mining and Metallurgy* paid foreign born miners a backhanded compliment in an editorial. "The Herrin mob, if we may rely on the newspaper reports, was not composed of the sort of citizens who are frequently characterized as huns, bohunks and wops. The names of the persons appearing in the newspapers had an old-fashioned American flavor."[3]

Almost all the outrage was directed at the miners and murders, but there were some exceptions. The Illinois Farmer-Labor Party channeled its outrage towards the Illinois Chamber of Commerce and its "relentless 'open shop' campaign to crush organized labor." The miners, according to the party's resolution, were "driven by savage oppression and the cold-blooded murder of their brothers by hired gunmen—the scum of Chicago slums—to defend themselves, their homes and their women and children by whatever means came to hand." Expressions of sympathy for the miners were rare, or at least rarely expressed in public. Even the *Ottawa Free Trader Journal* in Illinois, which proudly displayed a larger than average logo of the Typographical Union at the top of its editorial page, condemned Herrin as "a scandal to the civilized world," blaming the violence on "non-assimilable" foreigners "however lame it may be as an excuse."

One exception was the editorial page of the *Williamson County Miner*. The newspaper reported that "3,000 armed citizens" confronted the strikebreakers to secure "the future peace of their county." "There were no riots, merely the citizens of the county acting in the only way left them for the safety of their homes. The faces of the men who were killed in the disturbance are horrible sights. Uncouth, as all crooks must be in the beginning, they were doubly unattractive as seen after justice triumphed and the county had again resumed its normal peace-time behavior."

Collier's magazine reserved part of its ire as business people reluctant to testify because it might hurt their business. In "How Can Murder Help Business" the magazine wrote: "Those who read history will recognize this as the ancient frame of mind against which and in spite of which, law and order have been fought into being. Free government cannot last long in a community where men dare not testify against and punish murder. That

The Herrin Massacre of 1922

cowardice has made desolate tyrannies in some of the best lands of Africa and Asia. Our United States is not in that class."

The first reaction of Len Small, still on trial in Waukegan on corruption charges, was to blame Attorney General Edward Brundage, who was personally leading the prosecution, "for keeping me here at the time, and away from the affairs as Governor." Small tried to assess the situation, sending telegram after telegram, but reports from Hunter and Thaxton, to the limited extent they replied at all, indicated the violence had passed. Small delayed any action including calling up troops.

Safe in his hotel room in Chicago, William Lester was shaken, as was his wife. He blamed the state for not intervening despite his pleas. In the *New York World* he was quoted as saying "this wholesale killing is to be blamed on the officials. It would not have taken place if troops were sent when I called for them. The officials are directly responsible for this terrible state of affairs."[4] Lester told the correspondent for the *New York Times*, "the miners are nothing but Bolsheviki and the county is absolutely without a semblance of law. That is why we are going to make them pay ... we are going to tax the lawless class of miners out of the county and make them bankrupt for the next ten years."

One thousand soldiers stood on alert in the Chicago Armory awaiting orders from Gov. Small to move out to Williamson County. Other units around the state were also put on alert. The Illinois Central railroad reserved cars to transport the troops south, as did the El trains to move troops within the city. Col. Hunter and Sheriff Thaxton continued sending reports that the hostilities were over. Small considered removing both of them from their posts but did nothing.

President Harding was in the White House preparing for a trip back home to Marion, Ohio, where he planned to spend the 4th of July holiday, when the news of Herrin reached him. The day after the massacre, he met with his cabinet. More than the violence, about which they could do nothing, they were concerned by the effect of the continuing coal strike. The federal government had no power under the law to prosecute anyone in Herrin or to directly intervene in the strike other than by informal persuasion. Secretary of Labor James J. Davis said "one of the unfortunate features of this deplorable occurrence is that the death of those men will accomplish nothing in the direction of the dispute. Surely no better argument can be advanced for the settlement of these disputes around the conference table than the dead bodies of America workmen who met a futile death in this outbreak. Surely in

7. Outrage

this civilized age questions of disputes between men and industries can be adjusted without resort to bloodshed." Harding's Attorney General Harry Daugherty was silent for the moment but his paranoid hostility to organized labor as a Communist plot was evident. Daugherty once claimed his Red enemies planted poison gas in a floral display next to a podium where he was speaking.

On his return to Marion, Harding addressed his hometown and the larger national audience at the town's 4th of July picnic. Turning to the massacre, the president said "the foremost thought in the Constitution is the right to freedom and the pursuit of happiness. Men must be free to live and achieve. Liberty is gone in America when any man is denied by anybody the right to work and to live by that work. It does not matter who does the denying. A free American has the right to labor without any other's leave. It would be no less an abridgement to deny men the right to bargain collectively. Government cannot tolerate any class or group domination through force. It would be a sorry day when group domination was reflected in our laws. Government and the laws which government is charged with enforcing must be for all the people, ever aiming at the common good."

Federal judge Arthur Tuttle used the massacre against the railroad unions preparing for their own strike. In an injunction against the union members from trespassing on railroad property in Saginaw, Michigan, Tuttle wrote "organized labor cannot have the respect of honest men until it wipes out the disgrace of the Illinois massacre. It must purge itself. By acts such as that of Herrin, organized workers put themselves outside the protection of the courts."

John L. Lewis' first reaction to the news, speaking from Cincinnati, was he and the union were shocked by the violence which they deplored. Lewis denied that his telegram to Sneed started the conflict. The country, he said, had been "infested with thousands of detectives and Secret Service operatives whose employment by coal companies depends upon their ability to provoke violence and disturb public tranquility."

His claim was immediately challenged by Dr. F.C. Honnold, secretary-treasurer of the Illinois Coal Operators Association: "If Mr. Lewis knows of any sinister influence that has existed or men in the employ of Illinois coal companies who in any way incited the Herrin massacre it is his duty to state the facts clearly and not make idle and indefinite allegations, as has been his custom in every such case in the past."

Frank Farrington said, "act of violence only stirs the public against us and make bitter enemies for us in places where we should have strong friends."

Alfred M. Ogle, president of the National Coal Association said "the pitiful part of all is that this would never had happened but for the blindly suborn attitude to the international officers of the United Mine Workers in refusing to accept the offer of the operators in the several states and districts to meet and negotiate wage contracts." Samuel Gompers, newly reelected unanimously as the president of the American Federation of Labor, first claimed that Lenin and the Bolseviks were trying to undermine America by destroying free labor unions in America. "I regret, yes, resent the resort to violence in the Herrin strike. The stake of the miners is on such a high plane of principal it must depend upon the solidarity of action but need not and ought not fall upon physical force." Upon further reflection the 72-year-old Gompers took a more parental approach: "It is like a family quarrel, you know. Sometimes when you get mad at your family, you say a lot of hard things and they talk back, but the affirmations of each side, even if overestimated, bring to the light of day the things for which each side is struggling and the grievances each side is nursing. You have a rattling good row."[5] "The rattling good row" of organized labor, including the massacre, did not discourage Gompers: "Every day I see a brighter and better outlook before me. I am most optimistic for the future."

Kansas Governor Henry J. Allen, the creator of the Kansas Industrial Court which attempted to control labor relations via a Draconian agency, told a convention of the National Hardwood Lumber Association that "in Kansas we have 10,000 miners on strike and 2,000 working in the mines. The 10,000 who are out do not molest the 2,000 who are working. Why? Because Illinois statesmanship has not yet dared to do what Kansas statesmanship did two years ago. In Kansas when we don't like a thing we legislate."

※ ※ ※

The day after the massacre two of the survivors arrived back in Chicago and began talking. Fred Bernard, the cook saved by his fraternal order brothers told the story of his improbable escape. He claimed that three bodies were weighed down with stones and dumped into ponds, an allegation never supported by other evidence. Another survivor Fred Macy, identified as a "full blooded Cherokee," was quoted by the Associated Press as saying, "They say run to fence. They raise guns. Me know what come. Me zig zag this way, that way. Me dodge bullets—jump fence."[6]

7. Outrage

One can only wonder if the quote was accurate or doctored to sound more like the stereotypical "Injun."

Maj. Gen. Milton J. Foreman, leading a military commission from the Illinois National Guard arrived in Herrin to access the situation. After talking to the sheriff, states attorney, coroner, Hugh Willis and others in town Foreman reported there was no point to sending troops after the fact. No operator would dare break the strike, and Mayor Pace gave Foreman his personal word the wounded strikebreakers in the hospital would be safe. The troops waiting in Chicago were soon demobilized. The commission made a report apparently lost in a 1934 fire.

A man from the Hargraves Secret Service came by train from Chicago to check on the agency's employees. A party met him at the train station and warned him to make himself scarce which he promptly did.

Also moving north were two men on foot spotted by a railroad crew.[7] One was dressed in blood stained shirt and overalls from a gunshot wound. They asked the crew for permission to ride on a flatcar. The strongly union railroad workers, on the verge of going out on strike themselves, were not fooled by the explanations the two gave for their situation: they knew they had encountered two scabs fleeing Herrin. Rather than hurt them or leave them by the tracks, the crew helped them into the caboose, laid them down on their bunks and washed and dressed the injured man's wound. When the train reached West Frankfort the two men were taken to a hospital. A week later a rail union official warned them that "in the future it would be better for you to keep your nose out of UMW business. Don't pick up any more strays."

On the day after the massacre there were reports of long lines of cars leaving Herrin and at the Carbondale train station at least 150 crowded the platform waiting for outbound trains. Reporters asked the men their names and why they were leaving but none would response.

Governor Small continued to monitor the events from his hotel room in Waukegan as his corruption trial was coming to a close. Small tried to place the blame for the massacre on Attorney General Edward Brundage for tying him up in Waukegan while he should have been in Springfield. "Governor Small is mistaken where the blame belongs," Brundage said. "I he and his friends had not taken $1,500,000 interest in public funds, he would not be in Waukegan now."

Small and the Illinois first lady Ida attended closing arguments, watching Attorney General Brundage present the state's case against him. The case went to the jury Saturday morning on June 24. Ninety minutes later the jury found him not guilty (eight of the twelve later received state jobs along with relatives of the judge). The jubilant Small family left for their home in Kankakee. They and their supporters celebrated on the front lawn of the family home. Just as the party was winding down First Lady Ida felt faint and had to be helped by her husband to her bedroom. With her family around the bed she died during the night apparently of a stroke. The governor had to be sedated. Expressions of sympathy flooded into Kankakee, even from opponents like Brundage. On the following Wednesday flags across the state flew at half-mast and the state called for a moment of silence at 3 p.m. as the first lady was buried. Granting his wife's last wish, Gov. Small commuted the death sentence of Ignatz Potz to life imprisonment. (Years later, George Ryan, another corrupt Republican governor from Kankakee, would commute the sentences of everyone on Illinois' death row.)

By Friday, the day after the massacre, the atmosphere in Herrin began to calm. On Saturday night around 11 p.m., a group of men appeared at the hospital claiming they were there to safely escort the wounded victims to the train station, but the staff turned them away. Later, State Senator Sneed visited the wounded in the hospital, including P.J. O'Rourke, to ensure them they would not be hurt. Reporters began flooding Herrin. By Monday Herrin Mayor Pace was trying to salvage the town's public image: "Our city is being condemned by the entire nation, though not one drop of blood was shed within its limits. Herrin is a peaceful law abiding modern city, not a flag station or a mining camp." Pace also argued that because most of the murders had happened near Marion it was unfair to name them the Herrin Massacre. The *Herrin News* echoed that view: "what happened last week was really a Southern Illinois affair. People had come from several counties ... and there was probably a rough element no one could control." The *Marion Daily Republican* listed the names and affiliations of the outsiders and warned residents about talking to them. "Don't believe all you hear," read the headline in the Marion newspaper.[8] "People in Marion hope that the world in general will not believe all they hear in regard to the troubles here." The *Marion Semi-Weekly Leader* resented the criticism of Sheriff Thaxton as a coward and incompetent: "That Thaxton erred may be proven one day, but such statements, made in hasty surveys by visiting city men and 'yellow journalists' who seek nothing but big type headlines for their papers, regardless of the truth, are hurting us the deepest." An informal boycott of coal from Williamson County appeared and remained in place for a time.

7. Outrage

Escaped wounded strikebreaker Vernon Wilson walked into the offices of Follett Bull, Lester's attorney in Chicago. Wilson said he and another strikebreaker, Cherokee Fred Macey, escaped the initial volley and fled zigzagging into the woods. As they were making their way thought the woods, someone shot Wilson in the shoulder. Bull said he had received letters with death threats daring the lawyer to come to Williamson County to inspect the property or file suit for damages at the courthouse.

One AP report from Herrin claimed that newsstands were pressured to remove out of town newspapers, but copies were available for a premium under the counter and in alleys, much like buying bootleg liquor. The *Herrin News* reprinted the article that ran in St Louis and Chicago newspapers. The hometown newspaper thundered: "parties who live in Herrin know this statement to be absolutely false." C.E. Tudor, owner of a newsstand, said no one had pressured him and that the price for newspapers had not risen. Out of town newspapers did get parts of the story wrong, including a claim that five local women had been beaten to death. A long-scheduled parade and carnival with amusement rides, sponsored by the Lion's Club across the street from the hospital where the wounded and dying were confined, was misinterpreted as a celebration of the massacre. Most residents were silent, but the *New York World* spotted a sign in the window of a barber shop in Carbondale. "Twenty-five scabs are dead, nine are in the hospital and the mine is closed. The striking miners' prayer was answered."

The area became a national curiosity. In July Thoreau Cronyn wrote a full-page article in the *New York Herald* on the history of "Bloody Williamson," opening the story of the Vendetta to the outside world and analyzing the character of the residents of Herrin. "The people are still distinctly Southern, in their speech, habits and cooking," Cronyn wrote. George E. Lyndon, Jr., of the *Brooklyn Eagle* wrote six long articles from the area, as alien to his readers as China.

During the finger pointing, the legal process in Herrin and Marion was already underway. The day after the massacre the bodies were removed from display at the Dillard building and taken to the Albert Storme Funeral Home for an inquest. As in most places of the time and many places today the job fell under the duties of the county coroner. A coroner is not the same as a medical examiner, and the post is often filled by a funeral home director. Williamson County Coroner William McGowan was neither. In his brief biography he said the thing in which he took most pride, other than being a native of Williamson County, was his service to

The Herrin Massacre of 1922

the Republican party. The 58-year-old McGowan had filled a number of elected offices, as well as working as a coal miner, a dealer and an operator of a small mine. At the time of the inquest he was still a member of the United Mine Workers of America.[9]

By law, the coroner's duty was to conduct an inquest to determine the cause of death, determine if the deaths were the result of a homicide and make a finding and recommendation to the state's attorney for possible prosecution. The Coroner's Jury Foreman was Joe Barrington, a union miner as were Louis Gibbons and Philip Noakes. The other three jurors included an electrician, a shop owner and a superintendent at a water treatment plant.

McGowan and the jurors examined the bodies laid out before them. Numbers had been attached to their bodies.[10]

1. C.K. McDowell. Three pistol shots in abdomen and breast.
2. Name unknown. About forty years old: six feet in height, weight, 180 pounds One shot gun wound in left breast: one pistol shot in left check.
3. Name unknown. Body found hanging to tree. About twenty-four years old: height, six feet; weight, 150 pounds; light hair. Pistol shot above left ear. Strangulation.
4. Name unknown. About 45 years of age: five feet eight inches; weight 135 pounds; black scar on left shin. Two bullet wounds in left groin; two in leg.
5. John E. Shoemaker. About 45 years old; five feet eight inches: weight, 150 pounds; slightly gray hair. Pistol shots in neck and both arms. Body claimed by father and shipped to Charleston, Ill.
6. Name unknown. About 35 years of age; five feet eleven inches; 180 pounds; Shot gun wound in chin, two pistol shots in breast.
7. Emil John (card). About 45 years; five feet ten inches; 160 pound; bald headed. Pistol shot below right eye; gunshot wound in left hand and right leg; two pistol shots in left side.
8. Name unknown. About 38 years of age; five feet eight inches; light complexion, light brown hair; gun shot wound in left breast.
9. Name unknown. About 45 years old; five feet ten inches; with slightly gray hair; ring with red set on left hand. Shot gun wound in left side, left and right hand.

7. Outrage

10. Fred Lang, Chicago, Illinois. About 35; five feet ten inches. Pistol wound in left chest.
11. Arthur B. Miller, 1200 Madison St., Chicago. Illinois. About 30 years old; five feet eight inches; 145 pounds. Pistol shot in left breast.
12. Name unknown. About 40 years old. Five feet nine inches; 140 pounds. Pistol shot in lift side.
13. Name unknown. About 40 years old; five feet eight inches; 140 pounds; slightly bald; two gold teeth in upper jaw. Gun shot wound in right side; throat cut.
14. Antonio Molkovich, Groton, Russia. Two pistol shots in left side of body.
15. Nathan D. Overton, Poseyville, Indiana. Partly colored cross on left arm. Pistol shot in left side.
16. Name unknown. Pistol shot in breast and head.
17. Name unknown. Died in hospital. About thirty-five years of age; six feet in height; 180 pounds; gold teeth in upper jaw. Pistol shot in right shoulder. Throat cut.
18. Name unknown. About forty years of age; five feet ten inches; 150 pounds; scar from burn on body. Nine pistol shots in body; two in leg.
19. Howard Hoffman, 621 Webster St., Huntington, Indiana.
20. Jordy Henderson. Shot on Friday [sic], June 21, alleged [sic] by mine guards
21. Joe Pitchonis. Shot June 20 [sic] by mine guards.

The coroner's jury convened at the hospital to hear testimony from four of the wounded. Allen Findley had been a timekeeper at the mine. He testified that C.K. McDowell shot Gerodie Henderson with a high-powered rifle... "He was a good shot," Findley said.

Steam shovel operator Ed Green of Chicago said the Bertrand agent assured him the work in far distant Herrin was "was a fair and square job ... with the understanding that no coal was to come out." Green later tried to leave the mine but McDowell told him a guard would shoot him.

After a hearing additional testimony in the Herrin city hall the jury made its findings. The dead "came to their deaths by gunshot wounds by the hands of parties unknown." "We, the undersigned jurors," the report continued, "find from the evidence that the deaths of the decedents were due to the act, direct and indirect, of the officials of the Southern Illinois

The Herrin Massacre of 1922

Coal Company." Contrary to the jury's findings there were reports that McDowell had eleven bullet wounds on his body and that his skull was crushed including a hole most likely made by a pickaxe.

The coroner's jury's finding set off another round of outrage in the outside world. The report "would be a joke if any humor could be attached to the butchery at Herrin," wrote the *New York Herald*. It was, said the *St. Louis Globe-Democrat*, "as appalling and as menacing as the crime itself."

The adjournment of the jury and the release of the bodies left the fate of dead unanswered. McDowell's widow traveled to St. Louis, checking into the Hotel Statler. His 80-year-old father came to the Marion to claim the body under cover of secrecy after he was warned that even after his death the public's hatred for his son had not been satisfied. Where only a few months before he disembarked the train with a swagger the remains of C.K. McDowell were loaded in a freight car and quietly shipped to East St. Louis, and from there to his final place of burial in Colorado. The family also ordered the exhumation of his child for reburial next to him.

After his burial in Charleston, Illinois, newspapers ran a photo of John Shoemaker's widow and children, 7-year-old Audley and 9-year-old Jack. All three looked into the camera, more lost than mournful.

On Sunday morning, after the massacre, sixteen unclaimed and mostly unidentified victims were taken the potter's field in the Herrin cemetery. As a small group watched from the sidelines, a four by four grid of graves were dug by union miners. A procession of hearses and ambulances entered the cemetery, each containing a casket with the words "At Rest" cast in aluminum fixed upon them. Three Protestant ministers sang hymns and said prayers over the bodies. The small group of onlookers stood in silence as the dead were lowered into the ground. Small numbered tags were driven into the soil over the otherwise unmarked, undecorated graves.

The burials were not the final journey for some of the victims. "Grave No. 3" was dug up after Robert Anderson's brother and uncle arrived in Herrin looking for their missing relative. Their description matched one of the unidentified victims. The exhumed coffin was opened before the two men who recognized Anderson. His body was later shipped to Sparta, Michigan.

Other families arrived in Herrin to see if their missing loved ones were buried in the cemetery. After reading the descriptions of the victims in a newspaper Mabelle Jacobs of New York City wired ahead to the coroner to try to find her husband Raymond. The bodies were already buried

7. Outrage

by the time she reached town. Along with her brother-in-law she witnessed the exhumation of the grave and they both identified the body as Raymond Jacobs. The widow filed suit against Williamson County seeking $5000 in compensation as well as an additional $1000 for lost clothing, a watch and other personal property.

Arthur Miller's father arrived in Herrin from New York City. Like the Jacobs family, he had read a description in a newspaper of the body placed in grave 11. After exhuming the body, a mixup was discovered with the wrong bodies in the wrong graves. All 12 were dug up. After the confirmation of his identity Miller's body was placed on an east bound train.

Massacre victim Antonio Molkovich had served in the Great War. The Veterans of Foreign Wars of Chicago and the local American Legion post put up a large wooden cross over his grave, marking his service in the battles of the Somme, St. Michiel and the Meuse Argone, small towns in France as once obscure as Herrin had been a few weeks earlier but now household names forever linked with war and death. Molkovich's war record meant nothing to Herrin. The cross was vandalized and knocked over several times before the veterans gave up and the grave returned to its unmarked state.

Strikebreaker Ignatz Kubinetz, who died of his horrific wounds three months after the massacre, was put into one of the graves previously occupied by one of the exhumed bodies.

Other searches were unsuccessful. Benjamin Upchuch arrived in Marion looking for his missing son, rumored to have been killed in the two days of violence, although he was unsure if his son was with the miners or the strikebreakers, or just caught up in the middle.

A full week after the murders McCowan and a team of deputies searched the wreckage left at the mine for more bodies rumored to be buried there. The rumors were false, as were rumors of bodies dumped in lakes.

In sharp contrast to the disposal of the strikebreakers the two miners killed of the first day, along with Guy Bell Hudgens who later died of his wounds and then buried near Marion, were attended by thousands. Jordie Henderson's procession was led by a 20-piece band followed by 2,000 on foot. The white hearse was accompanied by the pallbearers marching alongside. A mile-long line of cars followed the body to the Herrin city cemetery. Joe Pichovich's funeral and burial at the San Carlo Catholic cemetery was proceeded by twenty cars loaded with flowers and 5,000 mourners.

The Herrin Massacre of 1922

In second week of July, *New York Herald* correspondent Thoreau Cronyn came to Herrin. Two railcars of coal set on fire by the miners were still burning. The mine's office was reduced to a concrete slab. Cronyn found shreds of cloth still hanging from the barbed wire fence and a shoe left by a fleeing strikebreaker on the ground by a tree. On one side of the trees were bullet marks. Some of the bullets had been dug out by souvenir hunters.

"Outside the old brick courthouse in the middle of the square," Cronyn wrote, "miners in blue shirts and overalls sit all day, waiting for the strike to end. They whittle and smoke and chew, and move only to keep out of the sun." Most people in the area felt, Cronyn wrote, "The less said the better: leave it alone and it will blow over and be forgotten."

※ ※ ※

Harding met with Lewis and Secretary Davis in the White House on June 26. Before the meeting Davis stated the miners should be punished to the fullest extent of the law. The only result of the two-hour lunch time meeting was the call for a July 1 meeting with the union and the operators associations. After foot dragging by the operators, prompting Harding to complain off the record "these Goddamned operators are so stiff necked you can't do anything with them," the parties met.[11] Harding warned that the government would take action to resolve the strike and urged the parties to negotiate in good faith.

"This is no time for the militant note of the radical who would prefer to destroy our social system, no time for the extremist who thinks the period opportune to break down organized labor. The government has no ear for either of them, but would gladly lend its cooperation to curbing the extremes of both," Harding said.

Hoover and Davis were delegated to oversee the bituminous talks, and Albert Fall was charged with the anthracite dispute. A week passed with no progress.

After returning to Washington Harding called Lewis and the coal operators to the White House. At the July 10 meeting Harding proposed that the miners go back to work under the old contract with the provision that Harding appoint an independent Coal Commission made up of representatives of all of the parties to study economic and other issues in the coal industry. Lewis rejected the proposed settlement. Governors of Minnesota, Wisconsin, Ohio and North and South Dakota then asked Harding to take over the mines and the railroads which were on the verge of going out on strike. Harding rejected the plea, but in a July 18 telegram

7. Outrage

to governors of twenty-eight coal producing states requesting the states to protect miners and operators and promising federal assistance if state efforts were ineffective. Individual operators requesting federal troops soon learned that the promise was less than it seemed, and that Washington would act only if the state authorities could not handle the situation and requested help. The coal operators continued to attack Harding, stating in its weekly industry publication *The Coal Age* that he had "hopelessly befuddled the situation." "In the panic over the coming shortage of coal the principals at stake are to be compromised. The operators are asked to surrender to the campaign of intimidations, terrorism and massacres that have characterized the union's conduct in this strike. For the operators to agree to President Harding's proposal would be not only to surrender on the points for which they have taken a stand, but to abandon the country to the rapicity of a strengthened, domineering labor monopoly."

On another front, the railroad strike dragged on. In early July three Missouri Pacific Railroad workers who crossed the picket line pulled into the Herrin station where they were scheduled to get off. The train was met at the station by three bands playing funeral dirges and a crowd of miners silently but intently staring at the train. The strikebreakers stayed on board.

After another month of foot-dragging on both sides, the parties reached the first of several state by state agreements to end the strike, keeping the old wage until April 1923, and the appointment of a coal commission. It was far less that what Lewis had hoped but under the circumstances the best he could achieve

※ ※ ※

Two days after the massacre Montana Senator Henry Lee Myers rose in the Senate chamber to speak.[12] Myers, a Democrat and a former judge, had been a longtime critic of organized labor. After reading into the record press reports from Herrin, which claimed a death toll possibly exceeding 40, Myers began by asking

> What was the offense for which these men were subjected to these frightful outrages, this terrible torture, for which they were beaten, shot, killed, murdered, hanged; shot down like dogs after they had surrendered and run up a white flag—40 or 50 men in a corral. attacked by 5,000 armed men, who, when they were attacked, immediately surrendered, ran up the white flag, and who were then taken out as prisoners and shot down when they were unarmed, defenseless, powerless? What is the offense for which this fearful, inhuman penalty was visited upon them?

The Herrin Massacre of 1922

Were they guilty of murder, arson, rape, burglary, treason to their country? Had these men outraged little girls, 10 or 12 years old, in their childish innocence, and then beaten in their skulls with clubs and rocks and thrown their dead bodies in thickets along the roadside? Had they outraged some virtuous matron and then cut her throat and left her to welter in her own lifeblood and await the return of her shocked and horrified husband, sons and daughters? Had they been guilty of burglary? Had they been guilty of murder or of arson? Had they burned down buildings? Had they damaged railheads or factories? Had they been guilty of larceny? No: none of these things.

Then of what were they guilty? They were guilty, each of them, of exercising the constitutional rights of every American citizen of working for a living, of earning an honest living with which to pay his honest debts and defray the living expenses of himself and family.

Senator Myers painted a glowing picture of the virtues of workers and bosses freely contracting for labor: "That is the offense for which this terrible crime was committed, horrible beyond description."

Myers compared the massacre to the German atrocities committed during the World War: "German atrocities of the World War horrified this country from one end to the other: but I doubt that any German atrocities were perpetrated during the World War that were more horrible, more shocking. more inexcusable than the atrocities of which I just read: and yet we call this free America, a land of liberty, a constitutional Government!"

Myers went on to squarely put the blame for the massacre on unions, "an invisible government, a self-constituted superior power, superior to human rights, superior to Government. There can be no free America until an American citizen or denizen can work at his calling or trade without having first to get the consent of an organized minority, a power which is more tyrannical and more domineering than anything else that has ever exercised tyranny and dominating power in this country."

Senator William Borah of Idaho then asked Myers to yield. The "Lion of Idaho" who as a prosecutor had faced Clarence Darrow in the murder trial of labor activist "Big Bill" Heywood, asked Myers if he knew where the strikebreakers had come from.

Myers answered that most of them came from Chicago. "[D]oes not the Senator think," Borah asked, "we ought to know whether these men went there in good faith or whether they went there merely at the suggestion of detectives as strike breakers?"

"I can see no evidence of bad faith in their going there," Myers said. "A man has a right to earn a living in this country. He has a right to go wherever he can find work. Two of these men were ex-service men. Two

7. Outrage

of them were college graduates. One of them was the son of a mayor of an American city. They were not all imported from Chicago. Some of them, it appears, lived in that part of the State."

Borah answered Myers that he agreed in principle that every American had a right to work and to be protected, "but the men who brought them in there—the operators—must have known from the experiences of the past that that kind of thing inevitably brings on just such affairs as happened at this place."

Senator Borah left the chamber as Myers continued to speak, launching an attack on labor unions as un–American. (Borah would return to Herrin in a 1923 speech using it as an example of how low civilization could fall in "the worship of force, this urge for blood.") After a time, Myers was questioned by Senator Holm Olaf Bursum, a Republican from New Mexico who filled a vacancy left by Albert Fall, who as Secretary of the Interior was then committing the series of felonies later to be known as the Teapot Dome Scandal. "[D]oes not the Senator believe" Bursum asked "that the fault for permitting such a horrible catastrophe was rather a deficiency in the public control by the constituted authority of the State in preserving the peace, rather than due to any legislation or influence exercised by any so-called organized minority?"

Retreating, Myers agreed there was much to the suggestion. If the state had done its duty, Bursum asked, taking the weapons from both sides, wouldn't that have prevented the massacre? "It is the fault of the State of Illinois in not going its duty," he said.

"Undoubtedly there was grave dereliction in the executive branch of the State government of Illinois," Myers said. "They will be derelict further in my opinion. In my opinion, nothing will be done about this matter. I do not expect any punishment of the guilty." No local grand jury, he predicted, could return indictments nor could the elected sheriff and prosecutor do their jobs. "It will be passed over; in my opinion, and will only tend to encourage and incite others to like crimes, in other instances, when they feel they have like provocation."

Four days later Senator Myers again spoke in the Senate chamber.[13] Clutching an editorial from the *Washington Post* from the day before Myers again blamed the union for the violence and ruefully predicted nothing would be done to punish the killers. "That act was one of the most horrible and reprehensible that has ever disgraced the annals of this country. It is anarchy pure and simple, ruthless defiance of the Federal government and State government, defiance of the Federal constitution and the

The Herrin Massacre of 1922

State constitution, defiance of all constituted law and authority," he said. "What is worse than the commission of the crime itself is that fact that the united populace of the county where it occurred appears to approve of it. The populace of Williamson County, Ill., appears to be unitedly and 100 percent disloyal to the United States and its Constitution." Herrin and all of Williamson County were in "rebellion," according to Myers.

> There is little room to talk about lynching in the South on account of heinous crimes so long as this sort of thing can be permitted to occur with impunity in other sections of the country and go unpunished. There is little use for us to talk about the atrocities of the Turks perpetrated upon the Armenians so long as a thing of this kind can happen in this country apparently without any punishment for it.
>
> If there be nothing done to remedy this awful wrong and to vindicate the law, either by Federal or State officials, I predict that it is going to create the greatest and most powerful wave of indignation amongst the law-abiding people of this country that this country has ever known. If the officials of the State of Illinois do nothing more than they have done, apparently, to uphold the dignity of the law; if they do nothing to punish this atrocious assault upon the constitutional government and upon the lives and persons of peaceful people, the State of Illinois will not be entitled to a place in this Union of States, and it will be a disgrace to the Union.

※ ※ ※

The July 1, 1922, issue of the *United Mine Workers Journal* had the usual front cover cartoon, pages in Italian and Slovakian and a back page written for women. The issue also recorded the union's official reaction to the massacre. "Mob Attacks Strikebreakers and Armed Guards at Strip Pit Near Herrin. Ill, and Many are Killed," read the factual headline above John L Lewis' statement on the "Herrin Horror."[14] He was both contrite about the violence while denying any union responsibility for it. "Thousands of detectives and Secret Service operatives," Lewis wrote, were employed by coal companies "to provoke violence and disturb public tranquility." He denied his telegram to Sneed incited any violence.

The official editorial in the mine workers journal condemned the massacre. "It is with bowed head that we write about the terrible affair that happened in Herrin, Ill., in which more than a score of human beings were destroyed in a lawless conflict." Ellis Searles, editor of the journal, reviewed the history of the union's fight for miners' rights. "It fought the powers of darkness and of evil with the weapons of education, enlightenment and honor." So much of the union's accomplishments were undone, he wrote: "The Herrin outbreak has given the coal operators the

7. Outrage

very weapon they were seeking with which to destroy the United Mine Workers of America. God knows the miners' union would not have had this thing happen for a million worlds."

The journal afterwards was largely silent, and Lewis made accusations against phantom Communists plotting the massacre and trying to destroy American labor unions as part of Moscow's grand plan. The next issue of the journal, dated July 15, did run a letter from a local union in Alden Station, Pennsylvania, reviewing the many incidents of violence, mostly unpunished, directed against unions and miners: "And if the rich and influential citizens of our country would guard against a repetition of the Herrin affair, let them begin by setting their own house in order and seeing that the full extent of the law is carried out when one of their number is involved just as energetically as when it is an outraged class of working men."

※ ※ ※

The outrage over the massacre took on an international turn beyond the worldwide condemnation. At the end of July, the Mexican Embassy in Washington filed a formal protest over the allegations that two of its nationals may have been killed in Herrin and another badly wounded. The protest was based on the statement of Jose Resendiz who along with his younger brother Francisco left Mexico to look for work. The brothers were on their way to Detroit but at a stop in Chicago they heard there were no jobs in Michigan but there were opportunities in Missouri, Kansas and Colorado. Along with two other Mexicans, whose names Resendiz said he never learned, boarded a train for St. Louis. On June 20 at a town "about 300 miles south of Chicago," whose name he didn't know, the four stepped off the train to get breakfast. Upon returning to the station a mob of about 75 men confronted them about what they were doing there. The mob accused them of being scabs and told them "to get ready for death." The mob fell upon them cutting and beating them with clubs. Francisco was largely unhurt, but Jose suffered wounds to his hips and face. Neither of the Resendiz brothers knew what happened to their fellow countrymen.

After escaping to Kansas City Jose gave the information to the Mexican consul. The embassy determined that the unnamed city had to be Herrin and that the missing, unnamed men were probably killed as part of the "barbarous and criminal" event. The Chicago consul requested State's Attorney Duty assistance, but he replied there were no identity documents on the bodies or surviving records to identify the men. An official from the

Chicago consulate travelled to Williamson County and was rudely turned away by uncooperative courthouse staff.

Harding's Secretary of State Charles Evan Hughes could do nothing in response to the Mexican protest except request that Governor Small do what he could.[15]

The Resendiz story is in many ways unbelievable. No one traveling from Chicago to St. Louis could accidently end up in Herrin, more than 100 miles south. They probably were there for strikebreaking. Neither Resendiz brother knew what happened to the other two men, much less saw their murder. The date is a day earlier than any other reported violence and it is unlikely one or more murders would have gone unnoticed. It is also doubtful that two corpses were slipped in with the others. The net effect of the Mexican protest was to bring even more attention and condemnation upon Herrin, Williamson County and the state.

In public Harding could do little and said almost nothing. In the Marion, Ohio, 4th of July celebration Harding, speaking before the hometown crowd that included his mistress Nan Britton, only mentioned "the right to work and live by that work." Great War commanding Gen. John "Blackjack" Pershing, speaking before Harding, also made a mild reference to the right to work in his address to the crowd without mentioning Herrin.

In August, as the Illinois Chamber of Commerce continued to raise funds for Brundage's investigation and prosecution in Williamson County, Harding wrote chamber president John H. Camlin that he only had "the public view of a horrible crime."[16] "It was extremely necessary to refer to the affair in my address to Congress because the general public did not seem to know that the Federal Government was powerless to act in the matter, and it was unbearable to have a widespread impression that the Federal Government was willingly or purposely ignoring that inexcusable crime." Harding went on to endorse the private fundraising for the state prosecution.

On August 18 the president addressed a joint session of Congress condemning the "Herrin butchery" and the recent abandonment of a train full of passenger in the desert by striking railroad workers.[17] He lamented that the country was at the mercy of strikers and that the federal government had limited power to do anything about it. Attorney General Daugherty saw the speech as a green flag. Using the Railroad Labor Act he obtained a restraining order injunction from federal judge James H. Wilkerson in Chicago against the railroad union basically stripping them of every right to speak or assemble, banning members of communicating by

7. Outrage

"letters, circulars, telegrams, telephones, or by word of mouth, or through interviews in the newspapers" any words to "encourage or direct anyone to leave or enter the service of the railroad companies."[18]

Harding's cabinet including Secretary of Commerce and later president Herbert Hoover were outraged. The cabinet meeting turned into a shouting match. In Congress impeachment proceedings were started against the attorney general. Under orders from Harding, Daugherty removed the offending language from the injunction in September.

Defeated but not silent, Daugherty delivered a speech in Canton, Ohio, in October. Addressing his many critics, Daugherty asked "where were these frenzied voices when that horrible thing occurred in Herrin, Illinois, that will forever be a blot upon the community and the nation?" "We had reached the time when, if necessary, people of this country, in order to protect their homes, perpetuate their liberty, and be guaranteed the right to work and earn and save, were about to be called upon to write in human blood a new Declaration of Independence and a new declaration of human rights and liberty."[19]

※ ※ ※

New Year's Eve, 1922, brought out the usual year end musings and reviews. Chief among them were the words of William Allen White. White was the editor and publisher of the Emporia Gazette in Emporia, Kansas, but from that small town spoke to most of America. First known for his editorial "What's the Matter with Kansas?" White's columns were reprinted all over the country, along with his numerous books for adults and children. The power elite of the country including presidents made pilgrimages to the Sage of Emporia for his common sense, Middle American wisdom.

In a full-page yearend review, reprinted in the *New York Tribune*, White focused on Herrin.[20] The town, he wrote,

> seems to be an average American town, not at all dominated by the foreign-born. ... The town folk did cowardly murder and probably tortured some of their victims. The union miners seem to have led, but they had the sympathy and support of their fellow citizens.
>
> It may be well to consider this butchery as something more than an outbreak of angry men. It may be well to ask why the men got angry; why they believed themselves justified in brutal slaughter of their fellow creatures; why the town stood by them. The men who were killed were only exercising their ancient constitutional right to work. Why were they treated worse than beasts? Americans are not given to bestial orgies like that at Herrin without some cause, however weak it may be.

The Herrin Massacre of 1922

We are facing here a changed attitude among workers and their sympathizers to our economic order. ...The latent right which the Herrin butchers supported was the right of a man to his job. Probably legally there is no such right. Yet here were a thousand men ready to risk their lives by murdering for that right.

Labor is beginning to feel that skill has the same status as property. Their right to apply their skill in the place where it will produce value labor seems to regard as an essential human right. This is astonishing. But we cannot ignore it.

This is a new doctrine and, being new, the probability is that it is false doctrine. But it has convinced men so that they will go to war for it. The cowards at Herrin were just like the German cowards in Belgium—kind fathers, indulgent husbands, ordinarily good citizens, mad with war lust, turned into mad dogs by fanaticism. And in considering fanaticism, after punishing and clearing away the fanatics, the thing to do is to consider its sources, to examine its bases, [sic] to see wherein the pressure of society on the human heart produces an inflammation that results in madness.

Herrin's brutes should be removed from society; but the thing that made them brutes; the cause that justified a whole American community in mob violence should be studied, and from this study we may learn a lesson.

8

Trials

People rarely need directions to the county courthouse. No matter how small the county or how impoverished the residents, the courthouse stands out. In smaller county seats, it is often the only multistory building in town, by its size an expression of what people want to believe about the majesty of the law and the supremacy of justice. Adorned with Greek or Roman columns, or ornaments from European castles, or a dome and a rotunda, courthouses of the era stood out from other buildings, surrounded as they often were by a public space with stone monuments, statues, Civil War cannon and park benches.

The Williamson County Courthouse in Marion had its own distinctive Italianate look. It was easily found by the out of town journalists and others vying for space to cover or just watch the trials of the Herrin Massacre defendants. For a time, it would be one of the most famous places in the world.

Almost from the beginning there were doubts that anyone would even have to answer in court for the massacre in court, much less face punishment. "Do Not Fear Punishment," ran the main headline in all capitals in the *Urbana Daily Courier* the day after the event, above the sub headline "Mine murderers may never be prosecuted."[1] It was not an isolated sentiment.

As the local and state prosecutors prepared their cases Harding addressed Congress on August 18.

> Had it happened in any other land than our own, and the wrath of righteous justice were not effectively expressed, we should have pitied the civilization that will tolerate it, and sorrowed for government, unwilling or unable to mete out just punishment. I have felt the deep current of the people's resentment that the federal government has not sought to efface this blot from the national shield, that the federal government has been tolerant of the mockery of local inquiry and the failure of justice in Illinois. It is the regrettable truth that the Federal Government can not act under the law. But the bestowal of the jurisdiction necessary to enable

The Herrin Massacre of 1922

Crowd outside the Williamson County Courthouse. waiting for news of the indictments, July 1922 (Williamson County Historical Society).

> Federal courts to act appropriately will open the way to punish barbarity and butchery at Herrin or elsewhere.

In the speech Harding also asked Congress for a new agency to take over the distribution of coal.[2]

The first step in prosecuting the murders of the massacre was the convening of a grand jury to consider whether there was enough evidence to bring charges against the accused. There was widespread skepticism that Williamson County would indict anyone. Shortly after the Massacre, Governor Len Small said, "a grand jury investigation in that county will be a farce. The murderers saw to it that there was [sic] no witnesses. Dead men cannot testify before a grand jury or appear on the witness stand." The National Coal Association among others publically bullied Small to take action. "The safety of every home is imperiled if such as crime is to go unchallenged and unpunished. Such murders have been flaunted by the international officers of the United Mine Workers as an example of what may be expected in other parts of the country if the operators and the American public do not bend the knee and bow the head in humiliation subservient to their arrogant domination," the association wrote Small.[3]

Attorney General Brundage, fresh from his defeat against Gov. Small,

8. Trials

perhaps saw a path to redemption by convicting the murderers of Herrin. After touring the crime scenes, he offered a $1,000 reward for the arrest and conviction of the killers. He spent his own money, beginning with $3,000, to finance the investigation and prosecution, and accepted funds from business groups from around the state intent upon punishing organized labor. The Illinois Chamber of Commerce began a campaign to raise funds for the prosecution. The *Illinois Journal of Commerce*, the Chamber's magazine, ran a map of Illinois on its cover with an ink blot labeled Williamson County. "What will you do to help remove this blot?" ran the headline. "The citizens of Illinois intend that the guilty shall be apprehended and punished, or that the full responsibility or non-enforcement of the law be placed upon the heads of those who control public sentiment and administration of justice in Williamson County," wrote chamber president John Camlin in a telegram to Harding. The president replied that as "the Federal Government was powerless to act in the matter," it was "unbearable to have a widespread impression that the Federal Government was willingly or purposely ignoring that inexcusable crime."

The business campaign to underwrite the prosecution gathered a reported $100,000. The state organization foolishly suggested the Marion Chamber of Commerce contribute $200, a plea instantly rejected. Colonel Hunter, speaking after the first trial, said the Illinois Chamber of Commerce induced him to fabricate false testimony that Samuel Gompers, John L. Lewis, Frank Farrington and other labor leaders were part of a conspiracy to attack the mine. Hunter said he told them to "go to hell." "My conscience is clear. I need make no apology to any man, nor fear that God condemns me. I did what was right in my mind."

Although Judge Hartwell had some involvement with the events leading up to the massacre, including warding off a mob looking to take his weapons by threatening to shoot them, and by meeting with local leaders trying to find a peaceful resolution, he would preside over the grand jury and trials. Judge D.T. "Dee" Hartwell took pride in being everyone's friend. After one year at a teacher's college in Indiana, Hartwell attended Columbia Law School in Washington, D.C., before taking the more usual path followed by attorneys at the time by reading in his father's law practice. After his admission to the bar he worked in private practice before taking the steppingstones of Marion City Attorney and Williamson County State's Attorney before running for circuit judge in 1915.[4]

Illinois Attorney General Edward Brundage bragged of his Horatio Alger childhood of hardship. By age fourteen he was "self-supporting" working in a railroad office in Detroit. Two years later he moved to Chicago and worked his way up to chief clerk. He studied law a little at a time before graduating from the Chicago College of Law in 1892. He worked his way up the Republican political ladder to the Illinois House of Representatives, and then to the Cook County Board of Commissioners, joining fraternal orders and four country clubs in Chicago and Springfield before winning statewide office.[5] On July 14, he took charge of the investigation, keeping Duty on the team. Brundage issued a call to find the identities of five key culprits including

Judge Dee Hartwell, ca. 1920s.

the pilot of the plane that dropped bombs on the mine. With his personal funds combined with the chamber's fundraising he aggressively pursued the investigation.

Duty told a reporter the grand jury would "clear the name of Williamson County." "I have a large collection of notes and Attorney General Brundage has a lot of evidence,"

On August 28, Brundage led the Special Grand Jury convened in the Williamson County Courthouse. He and Duty were joined by C.W. Middlekauff, a federal prosecutor and later by Thomas Mitchell a special indictment writer for the Chicago grand juries. Crowds surrounded the courthouse on foot and in cars, hoping to learn some news from the secret proceedings. Twenty-one residents, mostly farmers, which the *New York Times* correspondent said were "all Americans of the normal back country type of Anglo-Saxon-Celtic descent through the Southern Mountains of New England," made up the panel. Hartwell leaned back on his chair

8. Trials

placing one of his feet on the witness box. This is a job for real men, Hartwell said. The proceedings would forever be secret, and no blame could ever attach to them. "There comes a time in the life of all of us when a man will have to take a stand. If a man stands for the things he believes to be right, who can complain? I now ask you to go to your jury room to commence the performance of your duty as grand jurors." The panel, told by the judge that they could also bring indictments against the company for the deaths of the three union miners, retired to the jury room to begin hearing witnesses including the sheriff, the coroner and Col. Hunter, along with others.

Grand Jury proceedings were, as the judge promised, secret—more secret than information in the Pentagon. Exactly who testified and what they said remains largely unknown. One known witness was Allan P. Findlay, the timekeeper at the Lester mine, shot in the foot and left for dead with his hair tangled in the barb wire fence. Despite death threats slipped under his door in Chicago, Findlay appeared at the courthouse still limping from the wounds he suffered, protected by two guards. Brundage told a reporter from the *New York Times* that many witnesses the state called either refused to testify or claimed ignorance. "Some did not even know their neighbors," Brundage said. To get their testimony, Brundage threatened them with contempt or perjury charges. During a break in the proceedings examining witnesses Duty told a reporter, "the fear has touched many of them."[6] "I have been trying to get an old man to talk. His hair is white as snow and he saw things that day. But the fear has hold of him. He sits and swallows like a lizard on a fence. It is rather pitiful to see it." In all, about 300 witnesses were examined by the grand jury, which even met on Saturdays. At least one witness, Delbert Nelson, was arrested for perjury

Within a week the first indictments were returned by the panel, coming in bundles each day. A.W. Kerr, attorney for the defendants said the indictments bore "all the earmarks of having been drafted in advance by the Attorney General at 10 South LaSalle Street, Chicago, the Chicago address of the Illinois Chamber of Commerce."[7] In total 214 were indicted, 44 for murder, 58 for conspiracy to murder, 58 for rioting and 54 for assault with intent to murder. The grand jury report recited a balanced narrative of the facts, holding up Sheriff Thaxton's refusal to call for troops for special scorn "because of loyalty to the union or from fear for his candidacy."

The report said "the atrocities and cruelties are beyond the power of words to describe."[8]

After following the story from the surrender, the forced march, the execution and pursuit ending in the cemetery the jurors wrote "a mob is always cowardly, but the savagery of this mob in its relentless brutality is almost unbelievable."

As was its right the Grand Jury offered its opinion of the events. "Without discrimination, we feel keenly the horror of the tragedy. We protest, however, against the intimation that all of the people of Williamson County are lawless and un–American." The people of the county were responsible for those of its "supine, weak and cowardly officials who permitted the disorders to grow from the desultory rioting into a hideous massacre," but adjoining counties "contributed their quota of marauders." Notably absent from the indictments were any charges for the murders of the three union miners—no culpability was alleged against the Southern Illinois Coal Company.

The report included a familiar recommendation, as unfortunately futile then as now following mass shootings: "The ease with which firearms were obtained causes the Grand Jury to believe that legislation should be enacted to regulate or prohibit the manufacture or indiscriminate sale of firearms."

Many reacted with surprise at the indictments handed down by the grand jury. *The Outlook* magazine wrote that the grand jury "had faithfully and thoroughly done its duty."[9]

Throughout the region, the newly indicted defendants were apprehended, including Percy Hall taken into custody by his half-brother George Galigan. The Grand Jury had looked at more than the murders as evidenced by the search warrants issued at the time. One search warrant was directed against Oscar Greathouse and Luther Horsely for a generator, coils of electric and barbed wire and a copper kettle looted from the Lester mine. Wearing a brown suit with a yellow shirt and a cap pulled over his eyes, Otis Clark, accompanied by Frank Farrington, Hugh Willis, other state union officers and the defense lawyers, surrendered to the sheriff's office before he was confined to the county jail in Marion. Clark had been building a house when he was arrested. The Carpenter's Union took over the construction and finished the house for free. As the cells began filling others brought in less costly gifts, usually homemade food, for the prisoners. As the accused were taken into custody, they were processed by the already old fashioned Bertillon system, which allegedly could identify individuals based on a number of measurements of body parts, a process soon to be dropped in favor of fingerprinting.

Arraignment of the first 35 defendants began on September 25.[10]

8. Trials

Mayor A.T. Pace led a fundraising effort to secure bail for the accused. A group of 86 local residents, with a combined net worth of $10,000,000, put up $360,000 in bail secured by $720,000 in property. The 103,566 members of the Illinois district of the UMWA pledged to contribute one percent of their earnings for a defense fund. In the crowded courtroom, Hartwell called out the names of the sureties, much like taking the census he joked. The newly indicted defendants sat quietly in the courtroom, some accompanied by their wives and children. Eight defendants were denied bail: Otis Clark, Bert Grace, James Brown, Leva Mann, Phillip Fontanetta, Peter Hiller, Oscar Howard and Jess Childers.

On election day, the voters of Williamson County had their first opportunity to react to the massacre. Thaxton led all candidates in vote totals, defeating his opponent 9,150 to 3,426. Election officials noted a higher than usual number of split tickets voting for Thaxton, along with Democratic candidates. Farrington issued a statement after the election claiming a victory for the miners: "As soon as it became evident that the Illinois Chamber of Commerce, Attorney General Brundage and those who are attempting to use Herrin as a text for anti-unionism were intent upon defeating the Republican candidates in Williamson County, the miners rallied to the support of these men."

President Harding addressed a joint session of Congress in early December as the trial preparations intensified. America, he said, was more fortunate than other nations after the Great War. But for the rail and coal strikes "which had no excuse for their beginning, and less justification for their delayed settlement we should have done infinitely better." "But labor," he said, "was insistent on holding on to the war heights and heedless forces of reaction sought the pre-war levels, and both were wrong."

"I wish I could bring to you the precise recommendation for the prevention of strikes which threaten the welfare of the people and menace public safety." Harding lamented "an impotent civilization and an inadequate government" that lacked "the genius and the courage to guard against such a menace to public welfare as we experienced last summer." With the federal government's admission, it could do nothing in response to the massacre the spotlight intensified on the little courthouse in Marion, Illinois.

A trial is the dissection of chaos. Using rules and procedures developed over centuries, its goal is to strip away the unimportant and the prejudicial, and separate opinion from fact to find the truth—what happened and who, if anyone, should be held accountable.

The Herrin Massacre of 1922

After some pressure to bring all 48 defendants listed in the indictment for the murder of Howard Hoffman to trial together, Brundage and Duty rejected the mass proceeding, which would have been practically impossible, and choose to narrow the focus, putting five defendants Otis Clark, Leva Mann, Peter Hiller, Bert Grace and Joe Carnhagi on trial.

The selection of a jury by both sides is often the most important part of a trial but often the least interesting. The jury selection took four weeks, a time the judge noted from the bench was surprisingly short. At times it took an entire day to pick one juror. Names of potential jurors were drawn out of a box by a blindfolded clerk. At one point, 30 men were assembled for examination. When asked if any of them wanted to be excused, all of them raised their hands. The state exercised twenty preemptory challenges, removing potential jurors, some of whom could have been removed for cause, including friends and relatives of Otis Clark, and another who had brought cream into the jailhouse to the defendants, and one African American. Otis Clark's third cousin, Charles McInturff, was picked for the jury, as was George Cox, Clark's third cousin, and E. Sylvester Webb, who wasn't sure if he was Clark's third or fourth cousin. Juror Sam Watkins' brother-in-law had once been a scab miner, and Nathan Pendland reported he once had a disagreement with the carpenters' union. Most of the twelve were farmers and only one currently belonged to a union. A total of 220 men were examined by both sides. The defense had removed eleven from the panel, most of them farmers. The identity of the proposed jury members was covered in detail in the local newspapers. There would be no shielding of jurors, as is common practice today.

The prisoners waiting trial in the county jail in Marion were treated to meals from local restaurants brought to their cells, paid for by the union.[11] They received cigarettes, cigars, newspapers and candy, among other gifts from supporters. A farmer brought them five pounds of honey and one pound of butter. Lizzie Clark made a turkey dinner for her husband and all of the confined prisoners. To amuse themselves, they established a mock court in the jail including a presiding judge. The men received a steady stream of visitors. At other times they listened to records on a donated player. Shortly after the trial began defendant Peter Hiller married Anna Campbell in the county jail. The Carpenter's Union finished building Otis Clark's house for free.

Carpenters also worked on Hartwell's courtroom for three days, moving the jury box against one wall, facing the counsel tables, with the judge's bench looming in the middle. Special seating for the media was

8. Trials

built, which included three dedicated telegraphic lines. Additional spittoons were placed around the room. An observer noted the constant rhythm of wads of chewing tobacco hitting the cuspidors during the trial.

The first day of the trial, the doors opened at 8:30 a.m. and the seats were quickly filled, waiting for the 10 a.m. start. Judge Hartwell opened the trial with a warning: "There will be perfect order in this trial, and I will send the first person to jail who shows approval or disapproval of any testimony or statement during the trial. The attorneys will do the fighting. I'll do the ruling and no one else will help me."[12] He promised to bring in ten times the normal number of bailiffs if needed.

Delos Duty's opening statement outlined the facts of the case, laying out what the state intended to prove. For forty minutes he dryly outlined the facts of the case taking the jurors through the mine to the surrender and the march to the murder scenes. For another half hour he explained the law the jury had to apply.

At the defense table Angus W. Kerr, the lead counsel for the defense, sat between Hugh Willis and Frank Farrington. Kerr was a lawyer in Calumet, Michigan, when he represented miners in a copper strike in 1913. Taking up the defense of the striking miners he successfully fought the criminal charges brought against them. Kerr was hired the following year to head the legal department of the Illinois Mine Workers. In October 1914, 52 miners were killed in an accident in Royalton, Illinois. Kerr and his team fought for compensation for the victims' families and for the injured, wining more than the $300 first offered to the dead men's families. Kerr had only represented the union in civil proceedings until the massacre and he was reluctant to handle a criminal case. Despite his misgivings Kerr sold his house in Springfield and moved to Marion. Now with the other lawyers on the defense team and the five defendants crowded around them, Kerr rose and delivered his opening statement.[13]

The state, Kerr said speaking so quietly that many in the courtroom could not hear him, wanted to narrow the trial to the massacre, ignoring Lester's defiance of the strike and the introduction of armed guards. "They contend that no matter what events took place up to the time of the so-called Herrin rioting the actual issue now before the jury is what occurred in this one particular transaction which they have chosen to call the real issue in this case. With this contention we seriously disagree."

After reviewing the law of murder and the burden of proof, Kerr turned to the history of the miner's union: "No doubt many men on this jury will recall the days when the lot of the actual miner of the coal was a pitiful one indeed. No laws were upon the statue books to protect him, disasters that might well have applied to them the term of 'massacre' were of frequent occurrence in this industry. Human life was snuffed out in the gaseous recesses of the earth to the number of countless thousands." The single miner was powerless. "His voice was like that of the lost child crying in the wilderness." Operators cared nothing for the health or life of miners, nor for fair working conditions.

The miners, Kerr said, organized not just for themselves but for their children, "And in that battle, at every step, these determined workers were met with the powerful forces of organized capital. The miners lost. They lost again and again and again. But they persisted." The miners faced "private armies of gunmen" until they won. "And now in this case they are assailed for wanting to protect and conserve this organization," an organization Kerr said that benefits not just the miners, but their wives, children and the entire state of Illinois.

Kerr then turned to the facts of the case, Lester's agreement to remove the overburden, his betrayal, the introduction of strikebreakers and armed guards. Lester "went to the flophouses of Chicago, infested with the criminals of the earth. He went to the gunmen agencies of Chicago and there he recruited his army. It was an army of professional mankillers outside the law, with reckless disregard for the taking of human life."

Lester, Kerr said, did not bring the "army of gunmen" to protect property but to take the offensive. "You remember the miners were working in their gardens or corn patches or fishing in the streams. There was a Sabbath-like calm from one end of Williamson County to the other. Now, did this money-mad operator bring theses thugs in to protect his property or did he invade your county with an offensive army?" Kerr detailed 16 episodes of abuse by Lester's men, up to the killing of unarmed miner Gordie Henderson by C.K. McDowell, "the criminal—yes, murderous superintendent." With a Shakespearian cadence, Kerr repeated mocked the state's argument that Lester and victim Howard Hoffman were operating within the "Peace of the People" exercising their lawful rights.

Kerr listed for the jury 23 episodes of gunmen killing a total of 302 miners, beginning with the Homestead strike of 1892 to West Virginia in 1920. After each citation Kerr repeated "no gunmen were arrested." Williamson County, Kerr said, rose up in self-defense after the invasion of gunmen.

Kerr boldly stated that the killing of Howard Hoffman was not a crime.

8. Trials

> Even if you should by any stretch of the imagination find that the defendants in this case were there as participants, then in fact are they responsible for this? Was there no justification? Was there no excuse? Consider all of the circumstances.... Consider the unlawful entrance into the county, the unlawful attempt to mine coal, the unlawful bringing into this county this band of murderers, the only effect of which could be to stir up disorder, riot and breach of the peace, as we will show you.
>
> The killing of Hoffman was homicide and not murder. In some day and some court room a jury will say that the time has come in the industrial life of this nation to stop the importation into peaceful communities of this type of men. I believe that the day will come in this trial. I believe that it is this jury that will immortalize itself by freeing all communities for all time, from the sinister menace of the gunmen.

The people of Williamson County were the real victims, Kerr argued. "Men and women went about their ordinary pursuits without trouble and without discord." With the memory of "the terrible and trying conditions under which non-union miners worked" the citizens

> were peaceful and quiet, only awaiting a time when their employers would be ready to sign an agreement for work and again start the wheels of the coal industry. Into this community came these men, these scabs with all of the opprobrious meaning of the scab to such a community, come these gunmen, armed to the teeth with rifles and pistols and machine guns. They parade the streets and public highways, they close public roads, they arrest the progress of travelers and submit them to the indignities of searches and curses and abuse. They violate the peace of the community, they come like a horde of hired Hessians to invade and tyrannize and destroy.
>
> Above all, they seek to tear down the results of a quarter of a century of struggle and to reduce the coal miner to the dismal drudgery of the non-union fields. They seek to tear the little boy from the school room, from the sunshine and fresh air and throw him into the mine as a worker to toil and slave, an unwilling hostage to the greed of the employers.

The entire prosecution, financed by the Chamber of Commerce, was designed to destroy organized labor, Kerr told the jury. Witness after witness would prove the five men on trial were nowhere near Howard Hoffman the entire day of June 22, a promise Kerr would meet in the coming days. "Let the law be your guide, let the facts be your support and let justice be your product. We want nothing more." Kerr's opening statement was reprinted in a booklet called "The Other Side of Herrin," distributed by the Illinois Mine Workers and it remains the most potent defense of the Herrin Massacre to the outside world.

The state opened by calling witnesses to lay the foundation for the rest of the case, as basic as showing that Howard Hoffman was dead. Duty called coroner McGowan, undertaker Albert Storme and the doctors and nurses who treated Hoffman in the hospital before his death. Charles Hoffman testified that he identified the body of his son, using a photo of Howard in his Army uniform taken during his service overseas.

A series of witnesses brought bits and pieces of the overall story to the jury. One witness, a local real estate broker, saw Leva Mann leading the mob marching Hoffman and the other five to the cemetery. George Harrison and his son Fred testified how a mob chased the fleeing strikebreakers across their farm, the shots they heard and the discovery of the four bodies, one of which was hung from a tree and apparently used for target practice. Both father and son identified Bert Grace as one of mob carrying a revolver. They saw Grace get into a car that drove in the direction of the cemetery. Don Ewing of the Associated Press, perhaps the only outsider to witness the torture and murder in the cemetery, testified that Bert Grace prevented him from giving water to the wounded and dying men. "The first man to give them water will get the contents of this gun," he quoted an armed Grace as saying. Asked to identify the defendant, Ewing stood and pointed to Bert Grace.[14]

One key witness, William Goodman, did not want to testify against Otis Clark, his friend of twenty five years.[15] Goodman saw the miners leading the strikebreakers two by two to Crenshaw Crossing. He recognized Clark carrying a pistol not more than thirty feet away from him. Duty asked Goodman what Clark said. "I don't have to tell that, do I?" Goodman asked. Duty answered that he was under oath and required to testify. Goodman reluctantly repeated that Clark had called the mob to "stop the breed of them" and kill the strikebreakers. Goodman left the scene before the shooting began and walked to his brother-in-law's house in Herrin. During the trial, a UMWA officer visited the courtroom and reported on the proceedings to John L. Lewis. Otis Clark, he wrote, asked him in a "very pathetic voice" why John, meaning Lewis, had not been down to visit him.

Defense lawyer A.C. Lewis sought to discredit Goodman in his cross examination, questioning him on the time, his ability to hear what Clark said, and what Clark was wearing. Otis Clark was seen leaning forward, vigorously chewing gum as he conferred with the defense team. Goodman was nervous as he tried to volunteer information which prompted Judge Hartwell to admonish him several times. Lewis questioned Goodman about the weapon. "Where was this weapon?" he asked.

"In his hand."

8. Trials

"Where was the hand?"

"On him, just like it is today."

Goodman said he had visited the home of Leander Clark, Otis' father, about two months before the trial, but denied he told him "I don't know anything against Otis in this case,"

Another witness, George Nelson, watched Otis Clark and Oscar Howard pull McDowell out of the line and roughly take him away. As Nelson stood watching an armed man confronted him: "You go into your house so you don't know anything." Nelson heard the shots and later discovered McDowell's dead body.

A former mayor of Herrin testified about seeing Clark, Mann and Hiller at the various scenes. Dr. O.F. Shipman, an ear, nose and throat specialist, followed the death parade from his office to the cemetery. He saw Joe Carnhagi, Leva Mann and Percy Hall (who was not charged in the present case) torture the bound prisoners and shoot them repeatedly, Hoffman in particular. "Men, men, what are you doing?" the doctor said Hoffman said just before Joe Carnagi shot him again.

Robert Officer, the Ivy League graduate who worked as a bookkeeper at the mine, testified on the events, and how he survived by dropping to the ground, rolling to a fence and the running away. He heard someone call for the mob to kill the men, but he had lost his glasses and could not recognize the speaker.

P.J. O'Rourke, the only survivor of the public torture and murder conducted in the cemetery before a cheering crowd, took the stand. He was wearing an overcoat. Duty told him to remove it. "Going to make it hot for me?" O'Rourke asked. In a thick native Irish brogue he told his story of being marched out of the mine, shot twice at the fence, escaping to a farm house, his capture and being tied together with five others including Howard Hoffman and paraded to the cemetery. He testified how he was shot five more times. "We laid there about a half an hour. I asked for water and called out my mother's name and address and said to tell her 'I have gone.'" A man kneeled down on his wounded ankle. "I glanced up. He had a pocketknife. I then closed my eyes and felt him cut my neck." O'Rourke opened his collar and removed his shirt. He turned towards the jury, showing them the jagged scar that ran across his neck.[16]

Kerr asked O'Rourke only one question. "You were one of the armed guards who came down here?"

"Yes," he answered. O'Rourke was excused and the trial adjourned for noon.

Next to testify was another survivor Bernard Jones.[17] Jones had fashioned and waved the white flag. He and the others left the mine under the protection of the miners who promised safe passage out of the area. One man, he testified, demanded that all of the strikebreakers be killed. "I'll shoot them myself and take the responsibility," Jones quoted the man. Asked if that man was present in the courtroom, Jones stood up and pointed to Otis Clark. He continued his testimony telling of seeing Clark and another man lead McDowell away, and of how he survived the volley of fire and escaped with the help of a local resident who drove him into Herrin, where he eventually made it by train back to Chicago.

Unlike O'Rourke, the defense tore into Jones. Yes, Jones admitted, he was a guard as well as an investigator for the W.J. Burnes Detective Agency and a former railroad detective. "Were you called 'the rat'?" asked the defense team "Absolutely not," Jones snapped before the state could object. Jones was questioned about working in the Lester mine. "Didn't McDowell tell you to make trouble and shoot a scab if necessary to get the state militia here?" asked on the lawyers.

"That is not true," Jones said, slowly bearing down on each word. The defense lawyers continued to impeach his testimony until Hartwell declared an end.

William Cairns, another survivor, testified, identifying Otis Clark as McDowell's murderer.[18] Cairns was lined up with the others when the mob opened fire. He was hit with gunfire and fell. "As I fell I saw a big powerful man standing at the foot of a tree. He was bleeding and just stood there and yelled. Every time he yelled someone shot him again but he wouldn't fall down. A fellow came to him and said 'Can't we kill you, you big son of a bitch?' He shot him in the side and he fell." Duty asked Cairns if he could identify the man.

Cairns stood up and pointed to Peter Hiller. "There he sits."

Other witnesses for the state added to the story. That any of them testified was remarkable, in light of the threatening letters at least five of the witnesses had received at their homes. The judge released a censored copy, decorated with a skull and crossbones. "So if you don't go to Marion, Ill, in a few days and tell the court you told a lie, what will happen to you you will not know until it's to [sic] late," the letter read in part. Hugh Willis told a newspaper that the union officials had also received death threats, including some signed by the Illinois Federation of Grave Diggers.

Amid the blood and violence of the trial were moments of relief. During the trial spectators brought apples into the courtroom for the

8. Trials

accused. On one Saturday night the jury attended a performance of *Uncle Tom's Cabin*. Onlookers were amused as one of the court clerks began dressing like matinee idol Rudolph Valetino with bellbottom trousers and a wide belt. While the trial was underway in another part of the courthouse the county board approved a payment of $1,237.50 for the victims' funeral costs.

After its last witness, the state rested its case. The defense pursued a two-track strategy, one to expose the abuses of the guards and strikebreakers at the mine and two, to establish alibis for each of the defendants. The defense team called a long list of witnesses eager to testify.

The first issue was the closing of the public roads near the strip mine. The defense team called more than twenty witnesses who were either inconvenienced by the closing of a public road or harassment by the guards. Story after story of abuse by the mine guards were presented to the jury. The focus widened to the tales of guards terrorizing locals in their homes and fields, including 16-year-old Altha Davies at home alone with her seven-year-old sister as the armed men demanded milk and made suggestive comments.

Defense witnesses retold how the mine became an armed compound, and Lester's and McDowell's threats and defiance. When the fighting broke out on June 21 the jury heard how two union miners were the first to die from gunfire coming from the mine. Turning to the massacre on June 22 the defense produced more than twenty witnesses placing the defendants anywhere but at the crime scene. Perjury piled upon perjury. Joe Carnhagi was working in his garden and later hung out at a pool hall. Leva Mann was in a lumber yard. Otis Clark was riding around in a car at key times, far away from the murder scenes.[19] Bert Grace loitered on the public square. Peter Hiller was in a car with four witnesses.

The defense attacked George Nelson's reputation to discredit his testimony placing Otis Clark at McDowell's murder and the state in rebuttal tried to rehabilitate his testimony.

The defense was confident enough to waive a closing argument to the jury. The following day Duty spoke for two hours. "If these men had any part in the conspiracy, whether they fired a shot or not, they were guilty of murder. Every member of the Lester Mine Riot," as the massacre was already being called by locals, "whether they fired a shot or not. is guilty of murder."

"Facts can't lie," Duty told the jury. He reviewed in detail the evidence against each of the defendants and attacked the alibi evidence offered in their defense. One witness, Duty noted, who knew Otis Clark "from a babe" saw Clark lead McDowell away to murder him. Duty ridiculed the story that the mob members who came from other states were the main culprits.

"Those men when they left that mine didn't have all those guns you heard about." he said. "Some were bareheaded, some were barefooted and some had no shirts. Thet were lined up against a fence, defenseless and were shot down. These men were murdered. There are no mitigating circumstances. There was no self defense. It is only a matter of who did it. We have shown you five of the men who did it."

Duty then turned the jury's attention to the victim. "Howard Hoffman, the man for whose Death these men are being tried, was in the peace of the people. There were no mitigating circumstances in his case, no attack by him. It was the cruelest murder and of the cruelest kind."

"Gentlemen of the jury," Duty concluded, "do your duty when you go into yonder jury room. I am sure you will."

Both sides had offered more than the usual amount of requested jury instructions. Hartwell held up the stack of documents. "This is the biggest bunch of instructions I have ever had handed to me in my life. But for the sake of the records I've a good notion to chuck them all in the waste basket and give the case to the jurors without instructions." Hartwell ruled out a manslaughter instruction. "This is murder or nothing." The jury members retired to their deliberation room in the courthouse.

After the jury went out, the team of defense lawyers, headed by Kerr, issued a statement to the press. In it the lawyers said they felt no need to take the jury's or the public's time with arguments: "It is impossible to conceive how any fair minded jury which has heard this testimony can come to any conclusion other than that each of these defendant is not guilty." The lawyers reviewed the evidence, much as they would have in a closing argument: "The truth as it fallen from the lips of the witnesses cannot be changed and we have concluded to leave the facts with the jury and with the public with the sincere believe that a vindication of the defendants is prompt and certain."

After twenty-six hours and forty minutes of deliberation, in a room that had just had a padlock added to its doors, the jury returned its verdicts. Extra bailiffs stood guard in the courtroom and in the stairwells to prevent violence. The courtroom was already filled as Judge Hartwell entered, not pausing to remove his overcoat before taking the bench. "I am informed the jury has reached a verdict," he said. "Whatever it may be I do

8. Trials

not want you to express either approval or disapproval. I will not tolerate any cat calls or hissing or any demonstration of any kind. I do not want any weeping by relatives or any expressions of joy. I want that to extend all the way out of this courtroom and down the stairs to the street."

The jury filed in silently. The foreman handed the forms to the bailiff, who passed them to the judge. For all parties in a jury trial, the few moments this process takes seems like an eternity, as it surely must have that day. "We the jury find Leva Mann not guilty," Hartwell read, following with not guilty verdicts for Hiller, Grace and Carnhagi.

Otis Clark stood with his eyes closed. Judge Hartwell paused. Looking down at the form, he read, "we the jury find the defendant Otis Clark not guilty."

The courtroom was dead quiet as the crowd and the jurors left the room. The defendants, all of whom were held on other charges, were taken back to the jail by the deputies. The curious spectators around the courthouse walked away silently.

Brundage, who was absent during most of the trial and now speaking from Iowa, blamed the loss on the "spirit of intimidation that prevails in the Herrin district today." Frank Farrington said. "this was the state's best case and the verdict is a splendid one and very gratifying. Once again, the enemies of labor have been defeated."[20] Assistant U.S. Attorney Middlekauff said "a schoolboy, twelve years old, ought to know that this killing was murder and contrary to the law of the land." Although disappointed. he praised the prosecution witnesses for showing "as much bravery and courage as did the boys who went into the trenches in France." Kerr said, "if only the American public could be advised of the true facts as they fell from the lips and manner of the witnesses upon the stand no real American would disagree with this verdict rendered by the jury of farmers. It is the only and righteous verdict which could have been rendered against an army of invaders."

After the proceedings, juror Henry Riddle said six ballots were taken during deliberations. Some of the votes were close, except for the verdict on Otis Clark. The jury members stood around for several minutes. One of them asked "what do we do next?" before they went their separate ways.

The public reaction was predictably hostile and disdainful. The *New York Daily News* said "Herrin seems to be about to complete its secession from the United States of America."

The *Springfield Republican* of Massachusetts wrote that the acquittal was "the culmination of a bitter travesty of justice in the state of Illinois."

The Herrin Massacre of 1922

The *Chicago Tribune* wrote "Herrin is the portent of certain ruin to everything we cherish in American life. They will look back and see that democracy has fallen, not from the strength of an army but from its own weakness." In response to the *Tribune*'s editorial, William Potter of Marion wrote in a letter to the editor "we won the fight all right and can do so anytime your scabs want a battle. We got lots of guns and know how to use them." Despite the public's reaction or perhaps due to it Governor Small appointed defense counsel Kerr as a municipal judge for nearby Benton.

The second trial was quickly set on the docket. In this trial Hugh Willis, Otis Clark, Oscar Howard, Philip Frontanetta, Bert Grace and James Brown were accused of the murder of Antonio Molkovich, killed at the barbed wire fence. *Time* magazine, just weeks after its debut, wrote, "the second Herrin trial is on.... Again the lines of battle in the class war are sharply drawn: the zero hour is about to strike."

Much of the air had gone out of the second trial. There were few spectators and most of the media had left town. A jury was picked in half of the time, and it was again a panel mostly of farmers. During the trial Hartwell often stepped down from the bench, walking to different parts of the courtroom, sitting here and there, while continuing to preside. The judge banned shaking hands in the presence of the jury. One writer later noted that the defendants seemed bored and spent time sleeping or reading in the courtroom.

Assistant Attorney General C.W. Middlekauff delivered the opening argument, again laying out the facts the state would show. He did not defend Lester's actions but declared it irrelevant to the issues of guilt or innocence of the defendants now before the jury. The state he said did not represent Lester or scabs. "We represent the people of Illinois and your county."

In his opening statement in the second trial Kerr told the jury "we will show you who the real murderers in this case were, who came into this county with hearts malignant, filled with hatred.... 'We'll mine coal with blood, if necessary,' was the boast of Lester's crowd, and so they did." Lester and McDowell, Kerr said, "came into this county not to mine coal as miners do with pick and shovel, but with rifles and machine guns."

"Who were these people who came down here? Why Lester himself was a scab on his own class. He would not even join the operator's association. His army came from the flophouses of Chicago. They were not workers, reputable family men. They had no home addresses."

Kerr concluded, "you will be told that the eyes of the country are

8. Trials

upon you. Yes, but there are two sets of eyes. There are the eyes of those looking to the destruction of unionism. And there are the eyes of the poor and the oppressed who look to you to render a verdict in this case that will send the word out that the time has passed for the use of gunmen in industrial disputes in this country."

In many ways the second trial mirrored the first. Although the victim was different the witnesses and the testimony were much the same. Robert Tracy testified that Otis Clark called upon the mob to kill the scabs and stop the breed. Tracy then identified Clark by pointing at him. Tracy was near McDowell during the march to Crenshaw's Crossing. He testified that Clark hit McDowell in the ribs and head with a handgun. "He knocked McDowell back and I had to hold McDowell up to keep him from falling." Tracy said Clark grabbed the arm of the blood covered, exhausted man unable to continue because of his prosthesis. Cursing McDowell, blaming him for putting Alexander Howat in jail, Clark and Oscar Howard dragged McDowell away, as Tracy watched.

After hearing the shots that killed McDowell, Tracy testified that Hugh Willis arrived on the scene in his car and told the miners to move the prisoners off of the road and kill them all. Tracy stood and pointed to Willis at the defense table.

Otis Clark's long stream of alibi witnesses repeated the cynical mantra that Clark said he would have nothing to do with any violence and left Crenshaw Crossing before the shooting began. According to a parade of witnesses Philip Fontanetta was playing cards on the early Thursday morning while the massacre took place. Bert Grace, as in the first trial, hung out on the public square. James Brown, the only African American to be charged, had eight "colored" witnesses, as the local newspaper described them, place him far away in the small town of Colp, as did several white witnesses. Robert Drobeck, the editor of the Williamson County Miner newspaper, swore Hugh Willis never left Marion, as did several other witnesses. All together the defense called about one hundred witnesses.

Assistant Attorney General Otis Glen made the state's closing argument. "Someone was killed that day," He said. "The defense has spent several days in trying to prove that the killing of these men at the powerhouse was justified. Then, on the other hand they have produced scores of witnesses to prove that their men did not do the thing which they saw was the right thing to do."

As in the first trial, the defense was so confident it waived a closing argument. Judge Hartwell instructed the jury and sent them off for deliberations. Six hours and 55 minutes later the jury signaled that they had a verdict. The judge was waiting outside on the public square, ready to send the panel home at midnight when a deputy sheriff reached him.

After all of the parties were assembled in the dark courthouse, the jury entered. One by one, all of the defendants were found not guilty. The state asked to poll the jury, requiring every juror to stand and answer if he agreed with the verdicts. Two of the defendants tried to thank the jury but they were silenced by the judge.

The following morning defense lawyer Kerr requested an early setting for the next trial. Duty stood and said, "I'm not going to try any more cases. I intend to nolle [drop the charges] every one of these cases. It has been a terrible expense to the county. I have my personal opinion as to who did the crime and I tried to convince two juries. The juries have a right to their opinions and I am not complaining, but it's a hopeless proposition."

Brundage told the press, "the prosecution is reluctantly obliged to admit justice cannot be obtained in Williamson County. No impartial jury can be obtained to try the men responsible. Witnesses, reliable and trustworthy, at great risk of personal violence, have courageously testified to what they beheld on that fatal day, only to be impeached by witnesses who plainly were interested in the defense and who clearly were testifying falsely." "At this time," he added, "it seems that further trials would be farcical." Duty was more direct. "I am not going to try any more of these cases. Right or wrong does not make any difference."

The attorneys and the judge made post trial statements sniping, complaining and defending, the parties and actions, none of which made any difference. Those still in custody were released and charges against the long list of men indicted were dropped. Everyone accused or charged in the massacre was free.

During the trials from November 8, 1922, to April 30, 1923, the telegraph office in Marion transmitted 780,095 words to the outside world.[21] Local journalist Oldham Paisley, who covered the trials for competing wire services and newspapers, filed 403,000 by himself. At the end of the trials the cynical expectations had been more than satisfied and the public's and press's attention was turned elsewhere.

The *Washington Post* wrote

> It is a most deplorable state of affairs when justice fails so palpably and completely as in Illinois. The damage done to the State is incalculable. The effects of the loss of popular confidence in the State government are difficult to determine in all

8. Trials

their bearings, but no one can doubt that these effects are injurious to the prestige, welfare and safety of the commonwealth. The people of Illinois are living in the shadow of a terrible crime which their own courts can not avenge.

The *Springfield* (Massachusetts) *Republican* called the acquittal

> the culmination of a bitter travesty of justice in the state of Illinois. Yet the circumstances of the case are peculiar. The jury was composed of farmers living in Williamson county, where the massacre of the nonunion workmen took place. Farmers are not usually sympathetic with labor unions or with rough treatment of scabs and strike breakers. One is driven to the conclusion that the jury found the legal evidence against these individual defendants insufficient to warrant a verdict of guilty beyond a reasonable doubt.

Time magazine, which opened after the massacre, reported that justice could not be done in Williamson County. "This virtually marks the end of the Herrin episode." The observation was incorrect.

The judicial system was finished with the massacre but the legislative branch was just starting.[22] In March 1923, in response to a request for additional funds from the Illinois attorney general, the Illinois House of Representatives passed a resolution to investigate the massacre with an emphasis on how it happened and how it could have been prevented. A special committee was appointed by the speaker who named seven members, four Republican and three Democrats, two from southern Illinois, five from upstate. The committee quickly went to work, holding its first hearing on April 11. The committee members arrived by train in Marion on April 26, 1923, and took a tour by car of what was left of the Lester mine now again shipping coal under new ownership. They retraced the route of the miners and strikebreakers to Crenshaw Crossing, Moake's Crossing, the power house woods with the barbed wire fence, the streets of Herrin where the prisoners were paraded and finally the cemetery. The members felt the hostility of the residents of Williamson County, noting their absolute refusal to help and the widespread support for the murderers. In its final report the committee cited the testimony of Will Warder, a local attorney, who summed up the attitude of most people in Williamson County. "Lester was responsible for all that happened." The minority of residents who felt differently "do not go around making a big noise about it."[23]

The committee held hearings in Marion and Springfield, producing a transcript of testimony more than 1,400 pages long. Although the committee conducted an investigation into the facts of the massacre hearing for example the testimony of Patrick O'Rourke, the main focus was

The Herrin Massacre of 1922

not on what happened but on why it happened and how it could be prevented from happening again. The committee interrogated members of the county law enforcement who, with the noted exception of Delos Duty, were defiant and uncooperative. Newly elected treasurer Melvin Thaxton's lapses in memory were especially galling to the committee.

A key part of the committee's work focused on Col. Hunter's and Gen. Black's interaction before the massacre. Hunter claimed he had repeatedly warned Black of the looming danger and requested that troops be sent. Black denied it saying under oath that Hunter's reports to him were far less ominous and not calling for sending troops. Hunter believed that only local authorities could call for the National Guard, but under the law the governor had the power to send troops to keep the peace whether requested or not.

Hearing that the committee wanted to examine him, Hugh Willis fled to Hot Springs, Arkansas, dodging subpoenas. Willis sent word through State Senator and union official Sneed that he would only testify in Williamson County because of fear that he would be indicted for perjury in any other county. William Lester also fled the state. His Chicago lawyer refused to produce him. The committee heard testimony from others including his partner in another mine that Lester was repeatedly warned of the danger of attempting to break a strike in Williamson County.

One witnesses not heard in other proceedings was Gov. Len Small. Under a friendly examination, Small said he received reports from his secretary and Gen. Black as tensions built in Herrin. The decision to send troops into an area depended upon the need for them and the request of local officials if they were unable to cope with the danger. In 1922, the governor testified, he had received about 100 calls for troops, most of which were denied because they were unnecessary. "My time was very fully occupied with affairs in Waukegan," Small said. At 11 or 12 p.m. Wednesday night, he last heard from Gen. Black that the situation was under control. The first he heard of the massacre was an Associated Press report someone handed him in the courtroom. Small sent a flurry of telegrams to Thaxton, Duty, Black and Hunter demanding immediate replies for information, copies of which were entered as exhibits in the committee's record.

Small was the last witness before the committee. The investigating committee's authority was set to expire at the end of the legislature's session. House members fought to extend its existence, but as angrily noted in its final report, unnamed state senators fought the extension.

8. Trials

The impact of their action was that several witnesses the committee wanted to call including a deputy sheriff, a Herrin police officer, and a police magistrate evaded the subpoenas or left the county until the committee expired.[24] The committee condemned the law enforcement officers for casting "a cloud upon the citizens of that city and can only be removed by their being dishonorably discharged from their official positions upon their return home."

The committee's findings in its final report were blunt and direct. Melvin Thaxton, along with deputies John Shaffer and S.D. Storm, made not "one single move to prevent this trouble or to try to ascertain those responsible for the killings after the massacre lead to the conclusion that both the sheriff and his deputies, if not actually participating in the trouble, had full knowledge of the situation and sympathized with and acquiesced in the actions taken by those responsible for the killings." Thaxton was "absolutely irresponsible, incompetent and unqualified to hold any public office of trust or confidence in that or any other county in the state of Illinois." They were, in short, "criminally negligent."

Hugh Willis, the committee concluded, "could be convicted of this murder in any other county in the State." William Lester's actions were "one of the chief causes of the massacre," and "most foolhardy and unwise." The report recommended banning the employment of private armed guards during labor disputes.

Others including Fox Hughs, were criticized by the committee but special scorn was focused on the two officers of the state militia. Gen. Carlos Black had more than sufficient information to justify sending troops to Herrin days before the massacre. He was "derelict" for remaining in Springfield and relying on an inferior officer's observation and judgments. If he had done his duty, the committee concluded, "he would have called troops and averted the massacre." But more than anyone, the investigating committee found Col. Samuel Hunter to blame for the massacre. His actions were "entirely out of keeping with the facts and circumstances. No sufficient excuse is shown in the record for his failure to call for troops to handle the situation. We believe that he was absolutely incompetent, unreliable and unworthy to perform the duties assigned to him. We believe he is not qualified to hold his present position in the National Guard, and especially a position in the adjutant general's office where he might be called upon to exercise his judgment under like or similar circumstances."

A minority report signed by two members of the committee, while

The Herrin Massacre of 1922

repeating much of the majority report word for word, refused to single out Black or Hunter: "We are unable to definitely fix the responsibility, because of the mob spirit prevalent at the time, nor that there was any real or intended neglect of duty on the part of the public officials." The minority report was delayed because one of its members was in Waukegan representing one of the jurors in the Len Small trial, accused of rigging the jury.

The committee closed its work with a bitter denouncement of unnamed state senators who blocked the continued existence of the committee, which allowed key witnesses to hide until the expiration. "The committee hopes that these Senators will be replaced by men of high moral stamina and courage, who will think more of the protection of the fair name of the State of Illinois than their own selfish political ambitions."

On the same day, the committee issued its report Gov. Len Small exacted his revenge on Attorney General Brundage. Small vetoed the appropriations for four assistant attorney generals citing Brundage's ethical violations including hiring State Senator Otis Glenn as an assistant prosecutor in the Herrin trials. Brundage, Small wrote in his veto message, used public money "in a wasteful and extravagant manner and for partisan and personal purposes."[25]

"Early during the session representations were made to the general assembly that $75,000 was necessary to enable him to prosecute violations of the law in Williamson County. Newspaper mouthpieces of the sordid political faction represented by the attorney general were loud in their demand that money be appropriated for alleged law enforcement." Glenn, Small wrote, received $12,500 for the Herrin case but spent most of the time in Springfield acting as a vigilante for "vigilance in promoting his own finances out of the state treasury."

Hiring Glenn, who was rumored to challenge Small in the next primary, was unconstitutional as well as a financial abuse, the governor said. "In this case, under the guise of prosecuting law suits, none of which he won, the attorney general received money from the state treasury and instead of expending it the manner in which the legislature intended, he brazenly used the same, contrary to the constitution and very clearly for the political services rendered by one of his henchmen in the senate."

According to the *Chicago Tribune*, Col. Hunter, despite the public condemnation of his actions and inactions, fancied himself Len Small's running mate in 1924 and embarked on a tour promoting the governor.[26] On this campaign Hunter again failed.

8. Trials

In just over a year the judicial, legislative and executive branches of the state of Illinois, along with a powerless federal government, had completed their roles in the Herrin Massacre accomplishing nothing, changing nothing and leaving the system in the same disarray and disorder as before.

9

Prisms

Controversial events in America are often opportunities for individuals or groups to twist and exploit them to their own agendas or interests. Whether to attract followers, sell books, gain power, or just express their inner demons, a segment of the population is ready to couch and turn public events in their direction. The bigger the event the bigger the opportunity. For example, in more recent history, the segment of the public with a preexisting pathological hatred of government was ready to ignore all facts and reason after the federal government's actions in Waco, Texas, and after the terrorist attacks of September 11, 2001. The Herrin Massacre was a preview of this ugly aspect of the American character, at the dawn of the electronic revolution in media, as the events were viewed through their own prisms, refracting the truth into different versions, blinding them to anything out of their preconceived field of vision, even as they tried to lead others down their paths.

One of the more unusual analyses of the massacre came from Roland W. Harper, PhD, the staff botanist for the Geological Survey of Alabama.[1] In addition to plants, Harper studied and wrote about civilization. In a 1924 article "Civilization of Herrin, Illinois" published in the *Tuscaloosa News* Harper examined Herrin and Williamson County as civilizations by breaking it into quantifiable categories. Harper first examined the racial makeup of Herrin finding seven eights native white with the rest foreign whites "except for four negroes (two women and two girls) and one Chinaman." He noted that the small number of blacks in Herrin "seems to indicate that they are kept out by public sentiment rather than by the climate or industries." "The arbitrary exclusion of negroes itself points to a spirit of intolerance which is incompatible with the highest civilization," Harper wrote.

Harper looked at literacy rates, the size of families and property ownership. He began under the assumption that people without property had

9. Prisms

little to lose in violence but found that ownership in the county was higher than average. "This seems to indicate that there is not much to the idea, frequently expressed of late, that if more people owned their homes we would have better citizens."

One measurement of civilization, according to Harper, was inclusion in the book *Who's Who in America*. No one from Herrin was in the book and only two from Williamson County were listed. The county's rate of .006 per cent was far lower than the national average of .039 per cent. Harper placed great faith in the readership of certain magazines as evidence of civilization. Herrin residents outdid the nation by subscribing to the *Literary Digest*, a leading magazine of the time, 2.66 per cent over the national average of 1.98 percent. Readers in Herrin dropped the ball with lower than average subscriptions to the *Ladies Home Journal*, the *Saturday Evening Post, Country Gentleman* and *National Geographic*.

"Illinois is generally regarded as one of the most civilized states and it will be seen that Herrin is below the state average in nearly everything that counts," Harper wrote. "Although Herrin may not be the worst place in the country, and there are doubtless many excellent people there, as everywhere else, it apparently ranks low in most measures of civilization."

Harper concluded his analysis by stating "although it cannot be said that the lack of culture shown by the statistics causes lawlessness. It permits a state of affairs that would hardly be possible in a college town, for instance." He was later, sadly disproven in too many college towns in the 20th and 21st centuries.

※ ※ ※

Another somewhat unusual interpretation of the massacre came at the hands of painter Paul Cadmus. Cadmus was a courageous gay man at a time when just being homosexual was a crime. He was open and unafraid in his personal life and equally open and unafraid in his work, which he expressed with an unabashed joy. Cadmus was already an accomplished painter when he was hired by the New Deal program Public Works of Arts Project, part of the WPA effort to support artists during the Depression. In 1934, he was commissioned to create a painting for the Navy. Instead of the conventional depiction of military heroism, Cadmus delivered *The Fleet's In!* featuring a line of flamboyantly gay sailors carousing in a park. The Navy command was enraged, demanding the painting be destroyed. The Roosevelt administration, fearful of the kind of controversy the Rockefellers had brought on themselves by painting over a mural in the lobby of 30 Rockefeller Center, ordered the painting removed from public view, but not before newspapers ran photos of the work, usually with strong condemnation of how the WPA was spending the taxpayers' dollars. Cadmus became famous (or infamous) overnight.

Cadmus continued his work through the 1930s. In 1939, he and fifteen other artists were approached by *Life* magazine to produce a series of paintings on American history. Cadmus was offered the choice of the assassination of Huey Long, the Wall Street crash of 1929, the opening of the Panama Canal by Teddy Roosevelt or the Herrin Massacre. He chose the massacre and traveled to Herrin to see the sites for himself, although as he later said "I didn't follow anything very carefully."[2] After scouting the area and making preliminary sketches, he decided to focus on the torture and murder in the cemetery.

In his vision of the massacre, victims lying down along the bottom of the painting are remarkably free of dirt or blood staining their gym fresh physiques. One victim in a torn shirt pleads for his life as a man standing over him prepares to stab with a pitchfork. Another man seems to be clubbing the already dead or unconscious victims on the ground. In the background, another lays on the grounds of the cemetery as a woman in a red top and dark skirt prepares to step on his leg presumably on an open wound as actually happened. Less than a foot away another victim is standing next to a tree with a rope tied around his neck in either the first or final stages of being lynched. One of his tormentors is an African American. In the back of the painting is a close knot of men in the manner of saints in Renaissance paintings, some contemplating the scene before them, some indifferent, one laughing through his cigar. The arithmetic and geometry are wrong. There were six victims in the Herrin cemetery, not seven and none lynched there. The six were tied together, not left separate. The real cemetery in Herrin looks nothing like the painting nor is it laid out as depicted.

The finished painting was delivered to *Life*, which prepared the color plates to run it in the glossy pages. However, the magazine announced it would not publish the painting for fear of offending organized labor, a particularly hard statement to believe since Henry Luce's *Time* and *Life* magazines were vocal offenders and opponents of unions. In a 1988 oral history interview, Cadmus remembered that *Life*'s decision to withhold publication "wasn't a sort of national controversy, but people out there didn't like it." The painting appeared at an exhibit at the Whitney museum in 1940. Milton Brown, writing in the arts journal *Parnassus*, said "Of the

9. Prisms

164 pictures hung some are good, some are bad, but most are indifferent, and not one is really exciting, in spite of Paul Cadmus, who, as usual, makes an effort to produce a thriller but, as always, mistakes the sadistic documentation of horror for emotional depth. His Herrin Massacre will make your hair curl but that is about the sum of its significance." Writing for The *Arts Digest*, critic Payton Boswell, Jr., said, "From the standpoint of aesthetics and good taste I don't think it has any close competition for the worst example of so-called fine art I have ever seen." But perhaps he brought his own, small prism to the event—Boswell's father worked as a miner in Herrin before succeeding in the publishing business. The tempura on board original is on display at the Columbus Museum of Art in Ohio.[3]

※ ※ ※

The civil rights movement was still in its early days, even though the injustices which gave rise to it had existed for more than half of a century. Discrimination against blacks was a matter of degree, worse in the South but only by contrast somewhat better in the rest of the country. It was in fact Northern injustice which was the catalyst for the civil rights movement. The National Association for the Advancement of Colored People (NAACP) was founded in 1909 after race riots in Springfield, Illinois, the home of Abraham Lincoln, an obvious and shameful irony.

Through the "Jim Crow" laws, the overt segregation of schools, theaters, retail stores and public accommodations like hotels and restaurants, and the thousand large and small slights and indignities inflected on them, whites kept blacks in a permanent status as second class citizens. The South in particular added another weapon of terror to oppress blacks—the open and public spectacle of lynching. Lynching was more than hanging.[4] It was a community event, a team effort, a lesson not just to the condemned man but to any black man who might dare to look a white woman in the eye or show disrespect to a store owner.

While the vast majority of lynchings occurred in the South, they also happened in the North, including Illinois, as well. Belleville, Illinois, sits on the edge of the St. Louis metropolitan area, about 80 miles north of Herrin. Between Belleville and the Mississippi River lays East St. Louis and several smaller towns which by the turn of the century began attaching blacks from the South to work in the new industrial companies.

By 1903, enough blacks had settled north on the Illinois side of the

The Herrin Massacre of 1922

river to establish the village of Brooklyn as the first black majority community. One of its leading citizens was David Wyatt, a schoolteacher and principal. So it must have come as a shock when Wyatt was notified his teaching license would not be renewed by the County Superintendent of Schools.

On June 6, 1903, Wyatt travelled to the courthouse in Belleville to confront Superintendent Charles Hertel. Although it was a Saturday Wyatt found Hertel working in his office. In a heated exchange Hertel told Wyatt his license would not be renewed because of allegations of abuse against his students. Wyatt left the office.

Around 6 p.m., Wyatt returned to the courthouse, entered Hertel's office and shot him in the chest with a revolver. Hertel's secretary and his son grabbed Wyatt and held him until the police lead him away to the nearby county jail. The sound of the shot and the sight of a black man being dragged away from the courthouse set off anger among the passersby. As the crowd gathered the false rumor that Hertel had been murdered spread fueling the growing anger and calls to "lynch the nigger."

A self-appointed core of men decided to carry out the mob's wishes. Wyatt was safely locked in a cell behind secured doors. Soon the sound of the jailhouse door being battered by sledgehammer rang out to the streets. Small boys stood at open windows delivering progress reports to the crowd below. For hours, the mob worked battering down the doors and then the cell as Wyatt loudly begged for mercy or prayed to God. The mob broke the final cell door and swarmed over Wyatt.

He was dragged out of the building and into the street leading to the courthouse square. By now thousands were watching and cheering as St. Clair county officials including the state's attorney watched. Belleville police also stood by under orders not to fire into the mob.

Wyatt was dragged a few blocks to either a telephone or telegraph pole, where he was lynched. A fire was set under him and Wyatt's body was burned as the crowd cheered loudly. What little was left of him was taken to the dump. An estimated 10,000 people from all over region came to see the new tourist attraction.

Fifteen years later, in the town of Collinsville, a few miles north of Belleville, a white man was lynched. Robert Prager, a native-born German who worked as a miner in the area, openly expressed his Socialist leaning views that working people had no business fighting in the Great War raging in Europe. A mob whipped up by anti–German hysteria, in a region of strong German settlement and heritage, seized Prager and lynched

9. Prisms

him. No one was ever punished for Wyatt's or Prager's lynchings, a recent memory that may have emboldened the crowd at Herrin four years later.

At the time of the massacre, the main campaign by the NAACP and others focused on lynching, in particular a federal law to prosecute offenders almost never prosecuted under state laws. (A bizarre footnote to this campaign is on the pages of the NAACP's civil rights advocacy journal *The Crisis*. Borders of pages were often decorated with swastikas, at the time a benevolent symbol a year before an obscure beer hall based political movement in Munich, Germany would adopt it as a symbol of hate.)[5]

The focus of the campaign was passage of the Dyer Act. Leonidas C. Dyer was a Republican congressman from a St. Louis neighborhood with a large number of blacks. During the 1917 race riot that spread from St. Louis across the river into East St. Louis (an event well covered in other books in particular *Never Been a Time* by Harper Barnes), Dyer confronted lynching firsthand. He began consulting with civil rights activist W.E.B. Dubois and the NAACP to make lynching a federal crime. In 1918, he introduced the Dyer Anti-Lynching bill which failed. African Americans, still a forceful constituency in the Republican Party, urged an anti-lynching plank in the 1920 party platform.

Dyer reintroduced his bill in the House of Representatives. With Harding's public support, stating he would sign the bill if it reached his desk, the bill passed the House in January 1922. The bill stalled in the Senate because of southern opposition and by misgivings of the constitutionality of the infringement of states' rights. "Congress discusses constitutionality while the smoke of burning bodies darkens the heavens," read one protestor's sign.

The shock and outrage of the massacre took some of the oxygen out of the anti-lynching campaign. While the *St. Louis Star* newspaper shortly after the massacre wrote it was "in part an aggravated outbreak of the typical American lynching spirit," the victims were white, and the public seemed to care far more about them than the unfortunate blacks, killed mostly one at a time. The NAACP needed to refocus the attention back on lynching. The civil rights group noted in a statement the frustrations of the Harding administration "as an executive to deal effectively with the situation" of the massacre. "He frankly admitted that he was shocked to find that the government of the United States is powerless to protect the people." "Yet, how comparatively simple would have been the whole procedure had the Dyer bill been a law."

"The Herrin butchery," the statement read, should be reconsidered

The Herrin Massacre of 1922

in the context of a recent lynching in Dyersburg, Tennessee. A young man named Latin Scott was tied with wires and chains to a buggy axle and dragged. Red hot pokers were stuck in his eyes, and as he screamed, another red-hot iron was jammed down his throat. Other heated irons were placed on his body. As a crowd, with children hoisted up on their parents' shoulders, watched the stench of burning flesh filled the public square. A fire was built around Scott, but he held on to life for three and a half hours. "No, it was not the Turks murdering American Christians, nor the barbarians putting to death their enemies," the NAACP stated, "it was Americans torturing Americans, in America, witnessed by hundreds of other Americans."

The effort to one-up the Herrin Massacre had an unintended downside, turning the massacre back upon the anti-lynching campaign. Defenders of lynching who had previously kept quiet were emboldened to speak out. Yes, we execute criminals, they said, but unlike at Herrin we only execute the guilty. A letter writer to the *Chicago Tribune* named Jack Osborne, only identified as a Southerner without specifying a hometown, accused the newspaper of hypocrisy for condemning a lynching in the South (apparently referring to the mob lynching of Leo Frank in Georgia) while letting Herrin go unpunished. What was needed, Osbourne wrote, were "some real hemp parties" to restore law and order. In response to New York Senator William Calder's attack on southern lynching in the wake of two Africa Americans lynched in Georgia, Georgia Senator John Harris took the floor and said the South "should be left alone to settle its negro question. The good people of Georgia and the South deplore lynchings just as the good people of other States deplore them."[6] The people of Georgia were safer walking the street than people in New York City, he said.

Tennessee Senator William Shields joined the debate.[7] "He," referring to Calder, "did not say anything about the terrible recent massacre in Herrin, Ill. almost in the shadow of city hall in Chicago." Displaying as much ignorance of the facts as he did about geography, the senator said, "We don't know how many were killed, it runs anywhere from 25 to 40. These men had committed no crime.... And that it was out near Chicago and the local authorities have done nothing about it, and are not trying to punish these lynchers." The mayor of Center, Texas, G.H. Pullet, spoke for many in his letter to the *Manufacturers' Record*: "Had this occurred in the South instead of the North, we would have been branded by the Northern press as a brutal barbarous uncivilized people."[8] In a letter to the editor of

9. Prisms

the *Chicago Tribune*, W.B. Powell of Tavares, Florida, protested that the newspaper had attacked the South "because some dirty niggers have been lynched for an unspeakable crime against white women." He wrote "the lynchers of the south seldom, very seldom, get the wrong man and for a crime against the most sacred thing known: woman." D.C. Earnest of Dallas wrote, "we hang and burn Negroes down here for brutal crimes against women, but there is no instance on record where there has been wholesale assassination of men whose only offense was working for a living without first providing themselves with union cards."

By December 1922, the Dyer Bill was reported out of the Senate Judiciary Committee to the full Senate, where it ran head first into a week-long filibuster by Southern Democrats, led by North Carolina Senator Lee Slater Overman. Republicans reluctantly withdrew the proposal. "Good negroes of the South do not want the legislation" Overman said, "for they do not need it."[9]

Dyer would try session after session to pass the bill. He built public support but never succeeded in Congress. Lynching became less frequent, the reported cases dropping year after year. In 2005 the U.S. Senate passed a resolution apologizing for blocking the anti-lynching bills of Dyer and others.

※ ※ ※

One of the most cynical uses of the massacre came at the hands of John L. Lewis himself, turning the event against his rivals in the Illinois district, as well as the handful of Communist enemies in the labor movement. In September 1923, the United Mine Workers published a series of articles which were reported in *Time* magazine and the *New York Times*.[10] According to the UMWA the Bolshevists were intent on taking over America by infiltrating organized labor including their own union.

> Imported revolution is knocking at the doors of the United Mine Workers of America and of the American people. The seizure of this union is being attempted as the first steps in the realization of a thoroughly organized program of the agencies and forces behind the Communist Internationale at Moscow for the conquest of the American continent.

The Communist plot was, according to Lewis, "one of the best organized and most far-reaching campaigns in America that any country has been confronted with." The Reds had six thousand leaders directing one million members and sympathizers, according to Lewis, and received millions in funds from Moscow to finance the overthrow. "Immediately

The Herrin Massacre of 1922

before the start of the miners' strike on April 1, 1922 the sum of $1,100,000 was sent into the United States by way of Canada from Moscow for the purpose of enabling the Communist agents to participate in the strike."

"The massacre of the strike-breakers at Herrin, Ill," Lewis charged, "was engineered by these Communist agencies 'boring from within' the miners' union." Without a shred, of evidence he stated, "according to their own statements, they were engaged for seven weeks beforehand in their preparations for a tragic occurrence of this kind at some point in Southern Illinois as a means to arousing the workers to a revolutionary action."

The Third Internationale, the global arm of Communism, had already tried to overthrow the country during the steel strike of 1919, the railroad switchmen's strike of 1920 and the coal and rail strikes of 1922. Millions of dollars were allegedly funneled from relief efforts to finance the strikes. Leading this imaginary conspiracy was the very real William Z. Foster, head of the Trade Union Educational League, supposedly leading 67 Lithuanian Communists along with 19 other assorted agents of Moscow. Short of claiming that Martians used mind control rays from flying saucers, it was the least truthful story of the Herrin Massacre ever told particularly by those who absolutely knew it was false. After blaming the Reds for Herrin the articles went on to attack the Communist Party of America, the Workers Party of America, The Trade Union Educational League, the Friends of Soviet Russia and the American Civil Liberties Union. The supposed combination of groups was directed from Moscow by Lenin with a million members in 45 national organizations divided into 200 locals. The Red scare tactics had only one object—to allow Lewis to smear any opposition as Communist. Even by the standards of McCarthyism three decades later, it was absurd.

It was even too much for the Bituminous Operators, no friends of Lewis or the union.[11] John C. Brydon, president of a special committee formed after the massacre, said that there was no evidence of Communist involvement. "Herrin," he said, "is a perfect example of the flat untruth of the contention that any policy of the leaders of the United Mine Workers of America is the moving force that stirs, not foreigners, but Americans to unspeakable crimes against their fellowmen and against all those ideals which we think as proper to American life."

"It was no Lithuanian, it was John L. Lewis," who sent the telegram telling the striking miners that the men inside the Lester mine were "common strike breakers ... which preceded the barbaric march, ending in the massacre of the helpless men who had surrendered."

9. Prisms

The accusations against Lithuanians were disproven by the ordinary American names of the defendants.

> The names of the indicted men in the Herrin affair were names such as Otis Clark, Leva Mann, Peter Hiller and Burt Grace. Something closer to home than propaganda from far-off Moscow is the force which invades such American communities and transforms their inhabitants into men who indeed might have been fitting members of the gallant squad that executed the Czar and his family. That something is the deliberate policy of teaching men that might is right in labor disputes and that there are no rights except the rights of the organization which claims a super-loyalty and displaces all normal and natural loyalties.

The $17,000,000 raised by the UMWA in annual dues, Brydon said, "have a great deal more to do with the maintenance and growth of violence in the coal fields than the mythical $1,100,000 from the treasuries of the Soviet." The UMWA had raised $800,000 for legal defense costs, he said, in addition to paying $750,000 to buy what was left of the mine from William Lester.

Roger Baldwin, president of the American Civil Liberties Union, said "the latest discovery of an imminent revolution in the U.S. dug up by the United Mine Workers is the same old line of bunk." "We are not Communists"; Baldwin said.[12] "We are simply believers in unlimited free speech as the only guarantee of orderly progress."

In fact, the small faction of Communists in America was as shocked and caught off-guard as the rest of the country was. In a "Dear Comrade" letter to General Secretary of the Soviet Comintern Vasil Kolarov in Moscow, dated February 17, 1923, American Communists C.E. Ruthenberg and Edgar Owens reported on the party's activities in the United States.[13] After parroting the various nonsense about the overthrow capitalism and start the revolution, the letter writers closed the report by listing developments in which party members played no part, including a one-sentence statement about the massacre.

Another hard-line Communist dismissed the events in Herrin, as well as the entire American labor movement. James P. Cannon of the Worker's Party, speaking in November, told his followers that, in America, "we are not confronted with a revolutionary situation. The American workers are not class conscious. The think and act as citizens in society. The majority of them vote for the capitalist parties. The unions reflect this condition; they are reactionary and numerically weak."[14]

"You read about Herrin, Illinois," Cannon continued, "where a band of union miners slaughtered 18 or 20 scabs, and you think perhaps there is a revolutionary situation. But this is a mistake. He is fighting in defense of what he believes to be his rights."

Years later, author Alister Coleman showed a copy of the charges to an unnamed participant in the massacre. The miner, a veteran of the Spanish American war and the Great War, scoffed at the accusations. "Bolsheviki! If any of them Bolsheviki came down here we would treat them just like we treated them Lester scabs."[15]

If there was any justification, however thin, for the smear tactics, it came at the hands of the union's rivals, which attacked Lewis as a tool of capitalism. One vicious attack on Lewis came from Tom Myerscough, an open Communist and founder of the National Miners Union. In his self-published book *The Name Is Lewis—John L.* (which he sold for three cents a copy), Myerscough defamed Lewis with everything from colluding with the bosses to stealing elections, but did not mention a word about Herrin. In this one case, at least, the presumptive strike may have worked

※ ※ ※

Both the extreme right and left in politics attempted to use the massacre to their advantage. One group on the right was the American Defense Society, a group formed to promote American intervention in the Great War. The honorary president was Theodore Roosevelt, who was thwarted by the Wilson administration from forming another Rough Riders corps to fight the Germans. The society was strongly militaristic, supported the exclusion of socialists from the country, and advocated mandatory military service, a crackdown on sedition and above all the elimination of every trace of German language and culture from English-speaking nations. After the war, the Society joined the campaign against American entry into the League of Nations.

Following the massacre the Society wrote Lewis urging his cooperation in bringing the guilty to justice, the superficially friendly letter said "we believe that you, as a citizen, and in your capacity as the President of the United Mine Workers of America, have a duty and an opportunity to help maintain the supremacy of the law under which we live."[16]

Along with their letter to Lewis was a copy of their pamphlet carrying excerpts of newspaper editorial from all of the then 48 states attacking the miners, Lewis, the state of Illinois and the concept of collective bargaining. The pamphlet was widely distributed as part of the Society's outreach to Kiwanis, Rotary Clubs and Chambers of Commerce. "This wholesale assassination, committed under a flag of truce is without a doubt the

9. Prisms

most outrageous crime ever committed in the history of trade unionism, striking as it does the foundation of our Government," read the Society's cover letter in part. Members of the Society were urged to do their best to spread the word locally as part of the national campaign. In a letter to one of its members the assistant to the chairman admitted the campaign had been requested by the National Coal Association, but that the issues raised concerns for national security.[17]

Even the mainstream American Legion was tempted to take paramilitary action.[18] An unnamed correspondent from Ridley Park, Pennsylvania, wrote in a letter to the *American Legion Weekly*, "we are not hampered by red tape whenever and wherever there is a need. We are able to offer instant aid or independently to investigate and act and report. What finer tradition could be handed down to prosperity than that The American Legion helped stamp out mob violence from this land forever?"

Harding's Attorney General Harry Daugherty waited until 1932 before airing his views in the book *The Inside Story of the Harding Tragedy*. In prose both wild-eyed and child-like, Daugherty claimed the coal strike in 1922 was directed from Moscow which in a memo to Communist supporters in America urged infiltration of agitators and propagandists into the coal regions. "It is necessary to arouse striking coal miners to the point of armed insurrection," Daugherty quoted from the memo.[19] "Let them blow up and flood the shafts. Shower the strike region with proclamations and appeals. Thus arouse the revolutionary spirit of workers and prepare them for the coming revolution in America." As proof of the conspiracy, Daugherty noted that the memo was written before the April 1 strike date, something Moscow could not have known unless it was itself the mastermind behind the curtain. The truth is, of course, that the April 1 strike date was widely known and fully expected by all sides, including the many industries that stockpiled coal before April. As the strike proceded, Daugherty became more convinced of a Communist conspiracy, confronting Harding that the strike must be broken or "we must surrender to the gentlemen in Moscow who are directing it." "There were hidden forces at work that defied reason," he wrote.

Daugherty's book quickly went out of print. It was reissued in 1975 by Western Islands, the publishing arm of the John Birch Society, which is built on finding a grand conspiracy in everything in history, politics, the economy, education and entertainment, to name a few. Daugherty's dark conspiracies fit in well with the Society's worldview.

The left wing was even more inclined to exploit Herrin to further its

The Herrin Massacre of 1922

ideology. Within weeks a leaflet from the Workers Party of America appeared in St. Paul. Minnesota, praising the miners. "For once the workers put up a victorious defense." A year after the massacre came the book *The Government, Strikebreaker* written by Jay Lovestone and published by the Workers Party of America, a hammer and sickle proudly displayed on the title page. Lovestone was at the time an ardent Communist who would later turn 180 degrees to become an anti–Communist and eventually an informer and consultant for the Central Intelligence Agency.

> The story of Herrin is a story of the revolt of striking miners against the privately armed gunmen, thugs, detectives. The echoes of Herrin resounding from the press and pulpit, the legislature and schoolroom, are frantic shrieks merging into a hysterical chorus for barbaric revenge—for merciless retribution. Strikebreakers have given their lives on the altar of profits. The workers must pay. The must pay in blood.

Lovestone begins with a factual account of the event up to the point of the actual killings, where he claims nobody knows exactly what happened next and drops the story. Always on the side of the miners while rarely mentioning the union, Lovestone recasts the history into a struggle between capitalists and workers over the issue of open shops to break organized workers. He quoted Philip Kinsle, the "mouthpiece" of Attorney General Brundage, that "as the situation is developing, the murder charge will be lost sight of in the trial of the rioters, and the cause of the open shop versus union labor will be the central issue." Lovestone also made Herrin into a call for action on the issue in the 1924 elections.

Herrin, Lovestone wrote, is "part of the history of heroic resistance to the brutal tyranny of the ruling class. ...To the employing class life is sacred when it enhances profits. When life does not enhance profits it is worthless. And Herrin proves this beyond a doubt."

Another left-wing exploitation of the massacre came in an attack on John L. Lewis by the Socialist Labor Party booklet *John L. Lewis Exposed*, written by Eric Hass in 1937. Repeatedly calling Lewis a "labor faker," Hass followed the party line by denouncing Lewis' leadership of the Congress of Industrial Organizations. Lewis had kept Communists and their sympathizers out of the movement, inflaming the small number of true believers who wanted a revolution instead of better wages and working conditions. Reviewing the strike of 1922, in which the Socialist Labor Party claimed Lewis betrayed the workers, Hass wrote, "there was little violence except in Herrin, Illinois, where thirty miners were massacred and a score wounded in one battle," which was of course completely inaccurate but typical.

9. Prisms

Another left-wing use of the massacre appeared in the pamphlet *On a Labor Faker's Trail* by T.J. O'Flaherty, published in 1924 by the Workers Party of America. The focus was on UMWA Illinois district president Frank Farrington who was the target of a progressive slate in the next union election. Farrington's entire career was questioned and denounced as pro capitalist. The writer alleged that Farrington took a bribe from William Lester to keep removing the overburden, a payoff he split with Robert M. Medill, director of the Department of Mines and Minerals and another union official. The pamphlet also hinted that Farrington pocketed some of the Herrin defense funds. No evidence was offered, the disloyalty to the cause being more than enough to motivate radical voters.

※ ※ ※

Another unique view of the massacre came from Follett W. Bull, William Lester's attorney.[20] Bull had sued the UMWA on behalf of Lester shortly after the massacre. With a favorable decision from the U.S Supreme Court against the UMWA, Bull bragged he would bankrupt the union for the next ten years.

On September 24, 1923, Bull spoke before the Association of Life Insurance Counsel meeting in Milwaukee. He admitted he had little to do with life insurance law but at the urging of a friend he had come to tell the true story of William Lester. Lester, he said, had no intension of breaking the strike. Bull knew him for years as Cornell man in the coal business. After learning the business in Colorado mines, he opened his first mine in Missouri with Bull's legal help. Lester provided his workers with ice water but when the ice wagon was in sight but still five minutes late the ungrateful workers went out on strike. During the War Lester worked, he said, as a "dollar a year man" in Washington, D.C. With the armistice, he returned to manage a non-union mine in Pennsylvania. Bull did the paperwork for Lester's purchase of the Williamson County mine in 1921 and its creation as the Southern Illinois Coal Company.

At the start of the national strike on April 1, 1922, Lester hired union members with the union's approval to keep up the maintenance on the huge steam shovels. Later with union approval the overburden was stripped away, exposing some 60,000 tons of coal by June. Lester wanted to remove the coal only for the purpose of giving it to charitable institutions in Southern Illinois. Bull claimed the local official knew this and allowed the loading before changing their minds. Lester then bravely told them that some members were willing to work anyway and that union men with the steam shovelers would join them. Only then did he think of employing a few guards and other workers. Then "this thing" (the massacre), "struck them."

Bull assured the insurance lawyers the Williamson County people were "practically all American citizens of pure America descent." None of the atrocities they had heard about were exaggerated, but what was exaggerated were the stories of the mine guards' weapons for defense which consisted of one automatic rifle and no machine guns as reported.

Bull said Lester was in his law firm's office when the news of the ambush on the truck on the 21st reached Chicago. Lester returned to the Great Northern hotel and began trying to contact the governor, commanding general and Col. Hunter to ask for help and tell them the mine would be closed.

On the morning of the 22th Lester requested that Bull send someone from his office to go to Marion and take charge of the situation. Bull said

> I selected one of my partners, a long, lean fellow, who wore a blue suit of clothes, and had no idea at that time of what had happened: but I did hear that McDowell was in danger, and would not have charge of the mine, and I had had a telephone message from Lester, in which he had started for the mine, and Colonel Hunter told him to stop and not come there. So discovering that neither McDowell nor Lester were in the mine, I sent a word to my partner that he might take charge of it when he got down there. He says it was delivered to him by the Union Train Men, the envelope opened, and it unquestionably had been read. They watched him read it. He went to the hotel that night, and he said that somebody said. 'Why, the new mine superintendent is here, a tall, slim fellow with a blue suit on. Jim Connolly, the conductor on 67, said he was over here at the hotel.' Whereupon my partner went to bed promptly. They made it a rather unhealthy place, and he has cussed me ever since for my methods of telegraphing.

The partner, unnamed in Bull's speech, was Arthur S. Lytton.[21]

Bull then turned to a matter of even greater interest to his audience. He reviewed how the insurance companies covering the strikebreakers, support staff and guards were able to get away with paying nothing to the widows and orphans of the dead men, or to the injured. In leaving the mine under gunpoint the men were abandoning the job and that fact that they were killed miles away from the mine proved they did not die in workplace injuries. The Aetna Insurance company, in particular, was relieved from paying.

Bull previewed the forthcoming lawsuits against Williamson County and the UMWA. Sixteen days before the massacre, the United States Supreme Court had decided the case *United Mine Workers of America*

9. Prisms

v. Coronado. Chief Justice and former president William Howard Taft, writing for the court, ruled that labor union were subject to the Sherman Antitrust Act and could be held liable for damages, under the right circumstances that did not apply in the present, long fought dispute.[22] But the precedent now hung over all organized labor like a sword held by a thread. Lewis' telegram to Sneed, Bull proclaimed, made it "probably the best case which will ever come up for establishing liability against a Union for damages."

Easy puns about his name aside, Follett Bull's view of Lester as the ice water dispensing savior of coal starved charities is at best unsupported. The legal profession had its own interests and that of its clients to color or distort the truth.

※ ※ ※

But by far the largest and most successful use of the massacre came at the hands of the forces opposed to organized labor. "The effort to suppress workers' organization," wrote The New Republic in 1926 "is one of the most profoundly demoralizing tendencies in the United States of our generation." For them the massacre was a Godsend and a weapon they would use against labor as its power and influence declined during the decade. On the local and national levels the anti-labor forces jumped on the opportunity. Measured by the decline in union membership and power during the decade the anti-labor forces could claim a real return on their efforts.

The *Open Shop Review* immediately used the massacre as a vehicle to attack the very existence of organized labor. It ran a letter from "A Union Miner (but not by choice") from Lansford, Pennsylvania, describing how union members were intimidated into voting for a strike by forcing them to make a mark on a chalkboard as a "radical small-fry leader" stands by to force a vote in the yes column. "Those desiring to vote 'no' are scared away. They don't vote at all."[23]

Three weeks after the massacre, the *Manufacturers, Record* claimed "40 or more innocent men" were murdered in Herrin, long after the real number was known.[24] The issue carried editorials from newspapers around the country, including the *Louisville Courier-Journal*, which wrote" "unless the news reports have been incorrect there is no anarchy in Russia worse than that which prevails in Williamson County, Illinois. Bolshevism is blooded with crimes no more brutal than those which have befouled the coal mining region of Herrin."

The Herrin Massacre of 1922

One after another the editorials tried to top each other in condemning the massacre, with the true aim of attacking the existence of unions. The *Greensboro Daily News* wished for a Napoleon to end the Reign of Terror: "A couple of well-placed machine guns would have taken the enthusiasm out of the butchers of Herrin. A determination on the part of the Government to protect men who want to work, and if necessary to blow the life out of any and all who offer to molest them, would instantly end the reign of terror in all the coal fields."

The attacks continued for seven and a half pages of the journal, whipping the readers into a state of anger and hatred not unlike the miners experienced facing the strikebreakers but instead of weapons the labor opponents used public opinion and government action to suppress organized labor. To a large extent it worked. Labor union membership declined in the 1920s and neither party was willing to support legislation for union workers until the New Deal.

Even small towns in America had a Chamber of Commerce and at least one or more fraternal and service organizations. Mostly white, male, propertied and confident in the rightness of their belief in the virtue of free markets shed of government restrictions, the small-town burghers considered themselves the elite of the community.

The Chamber of Commerce in Ellwood City in Pennsylvania among many felt the need to weight in. "If these men who had a right to work and a right to live are not avenged America can do nothing but hang its head in shame whenever anyone mentions the atrocities of the Germans in Belgium or the Turks in Armenia." The Beckley, West Virginia, chamber said Herrin was only one of many incidents "where men have been interfered with in their pursuit of lawful occupations, by threats, intimidation or violence under the cloak of industrial strife."

Although they were largely preaching to the converted the impact of organized opposition to organized labor played a part in the public's image of unions during its decade of decline.

The *Wall Street Journal*, then as now a leading opponent of organized labor, saw an opportunity and barreled through it. The newspaper produced a booklet *A History of Organized Felony and Folly*. "Union labor is ever armed and equipped for warfare in the ambuscade of the barbarian." American labor history "is one of the most sordid records of humanity," which the *Wall Street Journal* was happy to retell beginning with the violent strike against the *Los Angeles Times*. A series of stories of past conflicts lead to the climax in Herrin, followed by some other incidents.

9. Prisms

The massacre, the *Journal* wrote, "was undoubtedly incited, whether willfully or not, by the national head of the coal miners, and was certainly condoned by the Illinois head." The smoking gun was Lewis' telegram to Sneed, reprinted in the local papers and read to the striking miners, leading to a chapter called "Unionists Mutilate Bodies." "Facing a handful of non-unionists, the population of Williamson County roared with anger; facing the aroused opinion of 100,000,000 people, the same population whines like a puppy." The largely factual account of the massacre was peppered with allegations that Lewis was the most responsible for the atrocity. Along with bloodshed, the *Journal* wrote, unions were responsible for high rents, low savings rates, public corruption, a decline in patriotism and high unemployment.

The massacre was a gift from heaven for the coal operators, fighting organized labor every day across the coal fields. Its response was the booklet *The Herrin Conspiracy*, published by the National Coal Association. The somewhat calm account did not prevent the operators from claiming "the murders grew out of what has every appearance—from the bare facts collected—of a well organized conspiracy." The booklet contains many allegations not found elsewhere or supported by other evidence including a claim that the word "scab" was burned on McDowell's body with a hot iron. Some allegations were at odds with the agreed testimony of many eyewitnesses including the survivors. Facts notwithstanding, the operators argued that the conspiracy was born "four or five days" before the well-planned assault put together by local mine officials, ignoring the raising furor and increasing violence as the events happened. The Herrin Massacre stands out from other episodes of violence by the path of its arc. In most episodes of violence there is a build up to the act then a de-escalation. In Herrin the day began quietly, grew steadily violent, escalated to the murder of McDowell, followed by the firing squad and pursuit, growing more violent as time passed ending up in the open torture and murder in the public streets and cemetery to the roar of approving witnesses. If there had been more strikebreakers to torture and kill, almost certainly they would have attacked. No conspirators could have foreseen it much less orchestrated it. But chaotic violence did not support the goals of the operators: a conspiracy of evil union bosses did. *The Herrin Conspiracy* was distributed throughout the country.

But while the anti-union newspapers like the *Wall Street Journal* and the array of anti-labor groups damaged unions and Lewis, they did not destroy them. In the following decade, John L. Lewis became a leading

The Herrin Massacre of 1922

figure in a new approach to union labor, organizing workers by industry, like automobile production, rather than by a skilled craft, like carpentry. The Committee (later Congress) of Industrial Labor or CIO broadened the fight for workers' rights and the forces opposed to them. One of many attacks upon Lewis and the CIO came in a booklet published by the Constitutional Educational League called *The Hell of Herrin Rides Again*. The 1937 booklet written by Joseph P. Kamp, screamed at readers about Herrin or "Lewistown" as it was renamed.

"Hideous Mass Murder in Cold Blood! Men hunted like beasts—shot down like dogs. The dying taunted, kicked and slugged. The captured tortured and then slain. The dead mutilated. Throats cut—bodies branded with hot irons—brains beaten out—necks stretched by the hangman's noose," the book begins. Kamp wrote that 47 victims "in a few horrible hours experienced a HELL on earth." In his version, which apparently was untroubled with accuracy or worries about plagiarism, Lewis knowingly turned an army of miners on the strikebreakers with the mission to kill them all. Kamp noted Lewis' absurd accusation that the massacre was a Communist plot led by William Z. Foster but claimed in the present campaign for the CIO Lewis had enlisted the support of the same William Z. Foster in an attempt to promote Communism in the labor movement. There would be more "Lewistowns" across America, more murders, more violence the booklet warned. But, of course, none of it happened.

Another attack on Lewis and the CIO came two years later on the floor of Congress.

Michigan Republican Clare Hoffman asked "who is the head of this Nation? Is it Franklin Delano Roosevelt or is it John L. Lewis?" Hoffman attacked Lewis and the UMWA for warning operators not to open non-union coal mines in Harlan County, Kentucky. Implicit in that warning was the threat of another Herrin Massacre which Hoffman reviewed in detail. "Does he [Lewis] expect that in answer to his statement that the mines shall not open, that no one shall dig coal until he joins the United Mine Workers; that those striking miners at Harlan, KY, shall shoot, hang or cut the throats of the men—citizens of Kentucky—who desire to exercise their constitutional right to work in the mines of that county?" Hoffman lumped Lewis, the CIO and the Communist Party into one force intent upon destroying the rights of free people going as far back as Magna Carta. Hoffman moved for a Congressional investigation of Lewis, which made the front pages across the country. Hoffman, who was a prominent

9. Prisms

anti–Semite and Nazi sympathizer, later went on to make his mark in history by standing against polio vaccinations because many of the doctors in the program had Russian names.[25]

The struggle between management and workers at times involved using the other's words against them. The Labor Defense Council, an organization of leftists including some open Communists, sent a fundraising letter in November 1922 to ask for support in its fight against the open shop movement and the prosecution of labor leaders in Michigan. The letter cited examples of government persecution of workers including "Herrin, Ill., the scene of a brilliant and heroic defense of union miners." It was the opening needed by the League for Industrial Rights in its monthly magazine Law and Labor to discredit the council and organized labor in general and mock the efforts to aid peaceful unions. Pro union groups and publications often cited the Chambers of Commerce and industry groups to prove the outrage over Herrin was a thinly disguised attack on all organized labor.

In 1923 in a conversation with President Calvin Coolidge Lewis answered his contemporary and futures critics, noting "in the past there had been numerous instances of miners killed by armed guards and gun men employed by operators, all without protest from the public. It was not the duty of the union to apprehend the murderers or to find out who was responsible for the murders. That is a matter for the public authority."[26]

※ ※ ※

But not every effort to use the massacre for political gain worked.[27] In 1939 Mitchell Hepburn, the premier of Ontario, Canada, attacked President Franklin D. Roosevelt for hypocrisy. Hepburn said that in 1922 FDR spoke out against Lewis and the Mine Workers in a post-massacre speech to the Elks convention in Atlantic City calling it "as atrocious a massacre ... as is contained in our annals. Men were killed, not cleanly killed, but brutally killed." Now, after Lewis and members of the unions under the new Committee for Industrial Industries had donated half a million dollars to the Democrats in the last election, Lewis was Roosevelt's great friend. In fact, the 1922 speech was by Assistant Secretary of the Navy Ted Roosevelt, son of President Teddy Roosevelt and distant cousin of Franklin, and the third Roosevelt to serve in the same, relatively obscure post in the government. Hepburn quoted the wrong Assistant Secretary of the Navy Roosevelt, a mistake very nearly made by the author.

The Herrin Massacre of 1922

Franklin Roosevelt apparently never issued a statement addressing Herrin but in his speech to the Democratic national convention in 1932 he denounced the 1920s as "a period of loose thinking, descending morals, an era of selfishness," an apt description of a decade that very well might have included the Herrin Massacre.

10

Aftermath

After the failure of the second trial of defendants and the decision to give up on any further prosecutions, Herrin and the surrounding area entered a period of even greater violence. Coal mining returned to its roots as a dangerous business marked by the deaths of 33 miners from a gas explosion on January 29, 1924, at the Crerar-Clinch Coal Company underground mine near Johnson City. Above ground, the open warfare between two rival bootlegging gangs, the Ku Klux Klan and S. Glenn Young, a violent criminal masquerading as a lawman, forever fixed the area's reputation as Bloody Williamson. There are many good books detailing the gang war in southern Illinois, which in the Anglo-American tradition of glamorizing criminals from Robin Hood to Bonnie and Clyde to Tony Soprano, is considered colorful and entertaining. While it is spoken of as a small town version of the Al Capone–Untouchable mythology (even appearing in a thinly disguised episode in the early 1960s television program "The Untouchables") in the act of being created in contemporary Chicago, the reality, like all real crime, was far less dramatic.

The Herrin Massacre and the gang war were related in location, a close proximity in time, and a handful of players, but were of very different natures. The massacre grew out of a conflict between workers at one location and one irresponsible boss. The gang war was the inevitable result of Prohibition, America's largest experiment in idiocy and insanity. The massacre did not create the gang war but perhaps it made unthinkable violence and the impunity of consequences a little more thinkable.

Almost from the day it became law, Americans began the widespread violation of Prohibition. It was no less the case in southern Illinois or in any other part of the state. Speakeasies and other sources of alcohol, some hidden and some quite open, sprang up overnight.

Some alcohol was locally produced by moonshining or home brewers and winemakers, but the bulk was smuggled into the area from Canada or

The Herrin Massacre of 1922

the Caribbean. One of the first to enter the trade were the Shelton brothers Carl, Earl and Bernie. Before Prohibition, the Sheltons were small time criminals. With the bootlegging soon came prostitution and gambling. Al Capone's organization controlled everything in Illinois north of Peoria, and the Shelton Brothers gang everything south.

One of members the Shelton Brothers gang was Charlie Birger, destined to become the anti-hero of the war. Born in Russia in 1881, Birger enlisted in the cavalry and served during the Spanish American War. After he left the army he worked as a cowboy. He ended up in Harrisburg, Illinois. His time with the Sheltons was short, splitting away to start his own gang. Birger took on the protection of Harrisburg in much the same way John Gotti would later protect his neighborhood. A robber made the mistake of hitting a store in Harrisburg. Birger personally compensated the owner. The body of the alleged thief was found a few days later. Birger regularly handed out money and food to the poor. He barred locals from his gambling parlor, telling them they had no chance playing the rigged games. Birger decided to expand his territory into Williamson County.

Opposing the gangs was the newly reborn Ku Klux Klan. The Klan of the 1920s for a time successfully rebranded itself as an advocacy group for people of white Protestant origin. In its promotional material the Klan claimed it did not hate Blacks, Jews or Catholics but would not yield the country or the culture to them at the expense of "true Americans." In 1922 Black nationalist Marcus Garvey reached out to KKK imperial wizard Edward Young Clark for support for his plan to resettle American Blacks in Africa. Racist and anti–Semitic attitudes were common in the country, for example customers in Ford Motor dealerships could buy copies of the virulently anti–Semitic Dearborne Independent newspaper published and distributed nationally by Henry Ford or buy his book The *International Jew* along with the latest model car. What set the Klan of that time apart was its anti–Catholic and anti-foreigner prejudices, preying upon fears that Catholics with allegedly divided loyalties to the Pope would take power. The crudest accusation against Catholics and foreigners was that they were somehow behind the liquor trade and trying to undo Prohibition. At its height of popularity, the Ku Klux Klan attracted millions of followers mainly in the northern states, particularly Indiana where it virtually controlled the state government. Klansmen openly marched down American streets, including a large demonstration in Washington, D.C. Some 5,000 people in Williamson County attended a Klan meeting in

10. Aftermath

1923. The large Italian and other immigrant communities in Herrin made it a natural Klan focal point.

The Klan brought in S. Glenn Young to enforce Prohibition. By some accounts, Young had been a guard at the Lester mine but had left a few days before the fighting started. Others disputed it, but Delos Duty openly called him a "scab herder." In the interim he worked as a Prohibition agent for a short time in the East St. Louis office. Young was fired for misconduct and was unsuccessfully charged with a murder. Young and his Klan henchmen started a reign of terror against the residents of the county, staging raids to search for alcohol and brutalizing average citizens. On one of the first bootlegging raids the authorities arrested Otis Clark. Young arrested the mayor and sheriff and declared himself the chief of police. Illinois National Guard troops. which may have prevented the massacre had they been called, were in and out of Herrin on an almost routine basis.

In 1924 the Kluxers took over the county government. Delos Duty had been shot and slightly wounded several times before losing to Klan candidate Arlie O. Boswell. Boswell had been part of the crowd in the Herrin cemetery watching the torture and murder.[1] In a shootout in a cigar store two months after the election deputy sheriff Ora Thomas shot and killed Young and two of his bodyguards before dying of his wounds. Young's funeral was attended by 15,000, many of them in bedsheets and hoods.

Hal W. Trovillion, publisher of the *Herrin News*, self-proclaimed as "The Coal Belt's Greatest Newspaper," decided to take action. With the support of church leaders, Trovillion invited nationally known evangelist Howard Williams to Herrin for a six-week-long revival. More than 160,000 attended the tent meetings. Gang members and Klansmen repented and publically asked for forgiveness. Businesses in Herrin shut down every day for noon time prayer services. Trovillion printed a booklet "Persuading God Back to Herrin." "Modern history does not record a community so completely God-forsaken as was Herrin and Williamson County before Williams came," Trovillion wrote.[2] In the introduction he made it clear the cleansing of Herrin's soul had nothing to do with the massacre. While condemning the "incident" with the "unpleasant title of the Herrin Massacre" he wrote "[b]ut that is now a closed incident. We are here concerned with the reign of terror that came later and from which the community is now emerging and which has little or no connection to the 'massacre' of 1922."

The conversions were short lived. Dead bodies continued to drop

The Herrin Massacre of 1922

throughout the county. One of the many killed was Otis Clark, shot down in front of his house on September 27, 1925, a few days after his forty-ninth birthday. His bullet-riddled body fell face up and he had a revolver that had been fired twice in his hand. Clark had been running a saloon in Herrin and apparently his murder was connected to a "liquor feud," as the newspapers stated. Six men were arrested for his murder. Fox Hughes, Mayor A.T. Pace and another local union official posted bond for the accused killers of their former ally.[3]

The Shelton and Birger gangs continued their war. Each side converted a truck into to an improvised tank. In November 1926, Shelton forces attempted an aerial bombardment on Birger's roadhouse and barbeque stand headquarters called the Shady Rest, just as an unknown pilot had dropped bombs on the strikebreakers during the siege of the mine the day before the massacre. Like that incident there are no further details about the bomber, whether it was the same pilot or a copycat. In any event the bombs missed and the Sheltons had to resort to old fashioned methods in successfully blowing up the Shady Rest.

During a temporary truce, the Shelton and Birger gangs combined their forces to target the Klan leadership. A Klansman tried to prevent Catholics including a nun from voting. What started as a fist fight escalated into a series of clashes leaving six dead.

Birger ordered the murder of West City mayor Joe Adams which two of his men carried out. All three were arrested and charged in Franklin County where Birger had no control. Although he did not pull the trigger Birger was found guilty. "They've accused me of a lot of things I was never guilty of, but I was guilty of a lot of things which they never accused me of, so I guess we're about even."

Birger was sentenced to death by hanging. The law at the time required public execution in the county where the crime was committed. A gallows was quickly built on the grounds of the Franklin County jail in Benton, in time for the execution scheduled for April 19, 1928. It was to be the last public execution in Illinois.

A large crowd had assembled to watch the show, craning their necks and raising on their toes for a better view. Neatly dressed in his best suit and accompanied by a rabbi, Charlie Birger stood on the gallows at the death warrant was read. "It's a beautiful world," he said. As he had insisted the executioner covered his head with a black hood instead of a white one so no one would think he was a Klansman. He stood erect as the noose was fitted around his neck. The command was given. The door beneath

10. Aftermath

Birger's feet snapped open and he fell straight down, suddenly snapping his neck at the end of the rope. The sheriff and three doctors made a show of confirming Birger's death and then placed his body in a wicker casket for a burial in a Jewish cemetery in suburban St. Louis. The crowd drifted away, some silent, some unable to stop talking about what they had just witnessed. It is impossible to prove, but also impossible not to believe that in the crowd were at least a few participants in the massacre. Perhaps the thought crossed their minds, as it should have, that if there had been true justice in southern Illinois it would have been their body dangling limply from a rope in a courthouse square.

After the execution of Charlie Birger, while his exploits grew into folklore and children reenacted the hanging with dolls and twine, the worst violence in Herrin began to cool off. The Ku Klux Klan membership dropped to almost nothing as the hoods and robes were tossed in the trash and millions repressed their involvement in Klan as an embarrassing episode best forgotten in a vault of silence. The massacre, or as the locals insisted upon calling the Lester mine riots, had already begun to fade. In Chicago in 1924, Nathan Leopold and Richard Loeb, privileged sons of wealth and education, murdered 14-year-old Bobby Franks solely for the fun of the intellectual challenge. Clarence Darrow in his 12-hour closing argument to the judge cited the violence of the war as a rationale for the irrational crime.[4] "These boys were brought up in it. The tales of death were in their homes, their playgrounds, their schools; they were in the newspapers that they read; it was a part of the common frenzy—what was a life? It was nothing. It was the least sacred thing in existence and these boys were trained to this cruelty." Darrow could have cited the more recent example of the Herrin Massacre, fresher in Leopold and Loeb's minds, where mass murder went unpunished. Leopold and Loeb escaped execution.

The very name Herrin took on a new meaning. Shortly after the massacre, *The Outlook* magazine wrote "Herrin, until lately obscure, has achieved infamy. That southern Illinois town has become known as the place where murder pays. Turks or Kurds who torture to death defenseless Armenians in order to rule the surviving population with a rod of terror can now enjoy the flattery of successful imitation in America. Perhaps Illinois will have added a word to the language. Nobody hereafter need mistake the meaning of the verb 'to herrin.'"[5] H.L. Mencken, who curiously had nothing in any record to say about the Massacre, which would seemingly would have been a natural target for his biting wit, did attack the commercial promoters in Dayton, Tennessee, hoping to cash in on the

The Herrin Massacre of 1922

crowds attending the Scopes Monkey Trial. "When people recall it hereafter they will think of it as they think of Herrin, Illinois, and Homestead, Pennsylvania. It will be a joke town at best, and infamous at worst."

In 1924, a correspondent for the *New York Times* visited Herrin. He found it a peaceful prosperous and friendly town despite its history. Why did so much violence happen there? He wrote that the answer goes "straight to the heart of civilization in this country. He who would understand America will do well to consider Williamson County, 'Bloody Williamson' during a half century. For this little tragedy-stricken city is America at its most promising and at its worst."

By the end of the decade, the Herrin Massacre had been eclipsed in the public's mind by the St. Valentine's Day Massacre as the most famous mass murder in Illinois or even, as measured by a body count, the worst massacre in the state and the worst of the decade. That it was inaccurate made no difference. The seven men machine gunned in a garage in Chicago became a pop culture goldmine creating dozens of versions of the event including a comedic one in the film "Some Like It Hot." The bullet riddled bricks of the wall where the victims were lined up were sold as almost sacred relics. In the mass market the massacre in Herrin had no chance. By contrast, the Lester Mine was bought by the Illinois UMWA in 1923 for $726,000 in settlement of the claims against the union and then sold for a dollar to the Caloric Coal Company.

Generations of children in Herrin grew up knowing little or nothing of the past except not to ask questions about it. The little spoken about it was defiant and unapologetic. Author John Boaz quoted "an old man" as saying, "I saw my father shoot a son-of-a-bitch scab, and later when he begged for water cut his throat like a Goddamn dog." Most witnesses or participants said absolutely nothing. The various locations of the massacre became like haunted houses places were children knew something bad had happened there without really knowing what exactly to be afraid of. The massacre was a blank space in local history with no plagues, no roadside historical markers, no Herrin Massacre Heritage Trail marked for Boy Scouts to hike and earn an embroidered patch. As late as 2009 the *Southern Illinoisan*, the leading newspaper in the region, still used the term "so-called Herrin Massacre" in a story recalling the event. The Williamson County Historical Society, which has done over the years an excellent and honest job preserving and presenting history, still refers to the event as the "Herrin riot" or the "mine riot." With the opening in 1933 of a simulated coal mine in the Museum of Science and Industry in

10. Aftermath

Chicago, millions have had a sanitized experience of mining, the closest any outsider would ever have of an industry creating so much death and violence on the front pages of their newspapers. In 1964, Illinois reached another symbolic reconciliation with coal mining by erecting a statue of a stereotypical miner, complete with a pickaxe resting on one shoulder on the grounds of the state capitol. The statue's sponsor was Paul Powell, a political powerhouse from southern Illinois, who upon his death in the 1970s, and the discovery of shoe boxes filled with cash, was found to have been a far more corrupt official than Len Small ever dreamed. In the end, the image of mining and miners were reduced to heroic or at least benign dimensions, far away from the hardness of history.

Starting in 1923, a more harmful force than the gang wars began in Herrin. It began slowly but grew until the results were undeniable by 1926. Before 1923, anyone who wanted a job could get it or change jobs in a few weeks. Many children left school after the eighth grade to go to work—no one needed a high school education to make a good living. Older workers who knew nothing but mining were secure and confident about the future. But then the technology of mining changed, with machines replacing humans, particularly in the loading operations. In 1928, the 1,800 workers at the New Orient Mine called a wildcat strike, unsupported by the UMWA, over the issue of mechanization. The strike quickly collapsed. Within months, 400 of the 1,800 miners lost their jobs. In 1930, miners formed the Committee for the Elimination of Mining Machinery, asking miners to refuse to use or fix machines, and calling for a strike. The effort failed and more miners lost their jobs. The smaller mines began to run out of coal that could be mined economically. Hours at other mines were cut. In the larger coal field, 34 mines failed in a two year period. By the start of the Great Depression in 1929, the decline rapidly increased. By 1939, three fourths of the coal jobs were gone along with 80 percent of the payroll. The peak of sixteen mines in the Herrin region fell to one. Around Williamson County a new feature, the "gopher mine," appeared like pockmarks on the landscape. Slapping together some homemade equipment, an old car engine and components salvaged from closed mines, the independent gopher miners dug coal by hand, producing just enough to survive. Without the coal jobs, other business collapsed. There were runs on the banks, which were forced to close their doors forever. Repossessions and foreclosures jumped. The houses built in town for the miners were torn down for scrap lumber. Schools remained open but teachers were laid off and those still working often went a year without pay in building crumbling for lack of maintenance or repairs. Seventy-one percent of the lots in Herrin were delinquent, cutting tax revenues just as they were most needed for relief. Local government operations largely ceased. There was not even enough funding to collect back taxes. Coal and the prosperity it once brought were gone with nothing in sight to replace it. At the lowest point, half of the people in Williamson County were on government relief. A Work's Progress Administration study, *Seven Stranded Coal Towns*, published in 1941, focused on Herrin and other towns in Williamson, Franklin and Saline counties. The authors used data from 1939 to diagnose how Herrin reached its state and how it might find relief. Both were bleak. "Within less than a decade the whole structure of prosperity lay in utter ruin. Where great noisy tipples had stood, one found a few years later only weed-covered railroad sidings, crumbling mine buildings, and scrub oaks growing in the silent mine yards."

A more gut retching picture of Herrin's fate came in January 1939. Around the same time the WPA researchers were examining economic tabulations, photographer Arthur Rothstein working for the New Deal's Farm Security Administration came to Herrin to visually document another part of America devastated by the Great Depression. In a set of sixty-one black and white published photos Rothstein recorded the once booming downtown now trying to survive with a little dignity. Unemployed miners stood together on the sidewalk, with nothing to do. Amid the slag piles and garbage dumps Rothstein found and photographed shacks built out of scrap lumber and old tin signs, the insides wallpapered with newsprint pages of advertising for expensive women's fashions. Some people stared into the camera. Others looked away, their bodies and faces tense with shame. Above all Rothstein made portrait after portrait of men only identified as unemployed miners, their faces a mixture of pride, pain and desperation. The prosperity that people had feared would be taken from them by strikebreakers from Chicago had been taken by the economy that had little need for Herrin or for them.[6]

However, even as the photos and the book were being printed new opportunity was developing. In 1936, the federal government began buying 22,000 acres of land south of Herrin. Three years later the government damned Crab Orchard Creek to create a 7,000-acre lake. The summer before World War II, the War and Navy departments decided to build a munitions plant near the lake. The complex sprung up almost overnight in a guarded compound of 500 buildings and 120 miles of roads. The Illinois Ordinance Plant, or Ordill as it was more commonly known, hired

10. Aftermath

10,000 workers in the impoverished region, producing a steady stream of shells and 500-pound bombs. The plant closed on V-J Day. The empty buildings and laid off workers attracted new investors like Sangamo Electric Company and Smoler Brothers dress makers. The Herrin Chamber of Commerce gave the Norge washing machine company free land to build a plant. The worse days seemed over. Marion secured another development, making its name synonymous with prison. From the time Alcatraz was closed until the new "supermax" federal prison in Florence, Colorado, opened, the prison in Marion was the unofficial toughest prison in America. Assigned to Marion were the worst words a convicted criminal could hear. It housed the most violent criminals that could not be controlled in other prisons and the most notorious organized crime figures and spies like John Gotti and Jonathan Walker. The community that could not do justice to the victims of the Herrin Massacre made a living dispensing it to others.

% % %

As part of the settlement of the 1922 strike, President Harding agreed to appoint a Coal Commission to study the problems of the industry and make recommendations for reform. The commission was at first widely praised and supported, including by Idaho Senator William Borah. The seven-member body was headed by mining engineer John Hays Hammond. Others on the commission included a former vice president, a federal judge, and the editor of the Atlanta Constitution newspaper and the director of the United States Geological Survey.

One group vitally interested in the commission's work was the Bituminous Operators Special Committee. Under the direction of attorney Henry Stimpson, FDR's future Secretary of War, the committee produced a 50 page report, directed to the public as much as the commission, on the massacre.[7] Herrin, the report said, "was due to no accidental, sporadic outburst of mob spirit." It and other disputes around the coal producing area of America were "pursuant to a deliberate, premeditated conspiracy, conceived and carried through to enforce the policy and monopoly of the United Mine Workers."

"What took place in Herrin was the logical and inevitable result of the establishment of the Mine Workers as a super-government in an American state." The "super-government" the committee wrote, took over the state of Illinois. "Murder is no longer murder in southern Illinois."

In a pastiche of a legal brief, the committee set out to indict, try and

The Herrin Massacre of 1922

convict the union for the massacre. William Lester was only exercising his constitutional right of property by bringing in replacement workers in defiance of the super-government. The super-government, argued the mock brief, organized and directed the violence without actually pulling the triggers. The report attacked the defendants chief among them Otis Clark for not testifying which Stimpson seems to have forgotten was his Fifth Amendment right. The report reimagined the death march of the six prisoners through the streets of Herrin to the cemetery as an act "in token of their subjection to the United Mine Workers of America." The report concluded that for a long list of crimes the UMWA was "GUILTY."

After a year, the Coal Commission issued its book length report. In one portion of the report the members focused on Herrin. Williamson County it wrote, was "an American community" of 54,052 "native born whites," 1,825 "negroes," and the rest "foreign born whites," 20 percent of whom were illiterate. It reviewed the cultural and economic history of the region: "Its people are intelligent, soft spoken, extremely religious, not given to profanity, and would resent any suggestion that they were not good, patriotic American citizens" How then did the massacre occur there?

When mining began, men were treated as less than animals. Working knee-deep in water in gas-filled underground mines, with no concern for workers health, men were paid as little as possible in the "ruinously competitive" mines, where "profit was the sole object: the life and health of the employee was of no moment."

"Then came the union," the commission wrote. Working conditions and wages improved. The union brought them "out of bondage into the promised land." The first loyalty of the residents was to the union, not the government that had ignored their suffering. The story of William Lester's intrusion into the union country was retold, including the "general terrorism" of the public travelling on roads near the mine. The commission examined the events of the massacre in detail with a sense of shock undiminished by the distance of a year. The commission flatly ruled out placing the blame on Communists or other leftists. Nor did it find the union, or the public officials of the county had planned the atrocity, although they might have prevented the massacre. The violence of the people, provoked by Lester, was "spontaneous and instantaneous," but by no means excusable. "If those indicted, tried and acquitted were not guilty, there must be many people in Williamson County who know who the guilty ones are. Yet, there has been no conviction for this breach of criminal

10. Aftermath

law, nor is there the remotest possibility there ever will be one." Defense of the union and the good life it brought to Williamson County overcame all other human impulses. To the commission the explanation was not a justification.

> The report examined how coal disputes in the rest of the country were different from Herrin, including something as basic as topography. Many mines were isolated, often located in the bottom of a valley with step hills. Miners there lived in operator owned housing with company stores that exploited workers and their families. "That they are ill advised, obnoxious and inconsistent with the spirit of free local communities hardly requires argument. Self-respecting Americans will find a way to put an end to them." The miners there lived under "feudal" conditions. Miners there fought for their rights from a position of powerlessness: in Herrin miners fought back because they had power.

Without naming the Bituminous Operators Special Committee, the commission found the statements and testimony furnished by parties as largely "absolutely valueless." That lawyers tried to pass off such materials as evidence was "somewhat remarkable."

After examining the history of several operator-union conflicts, the commission again turned to Herrin. There was "indisputable proof that three union miners were killed and that no attempt has been made to ascertain or punish the guilty parties. There is no doubt that what are commonly known as strike breakers, gunmen, or thugs were brought to that county thoroughly equipped with arms and ammunition and perfectly willing to shoot without provocation."

Like the courts, the commission wrote it could not find "ultimate responsibility for the destruction of life and property." The commission "would impress upon the law-making power of the land and the common sense of our people this ever-to-be-remembered fact: All justice is human and fallible."

The commission affirmed the right of coal operators to conduct business. It also affirmed the right of the United Mine Workers of America to organize miners and for miners to join the union. The conflict between these two sets of rights, which the commission likened to the Declaration of Independence's recognition that "all men are created equal" at a time when men and women were held as slaves with the legal status of livestock, was the crux of the problem facing the country. "A democracy that can not spell peace with justice will sooner or later be succeeded by a government that will spell peace regardless of justice."

As bold as the Commission was in examining the problems of the

The Herrin Massacre of 1922

industry, the set of recommendations were tepid at best. Finding the balance between labor and management would have to wait until the 1930s after further labor disputes and the passage of the Wagner Labor Act. Despite its careful and balanced analysis, the Coal Commission had little impact. Senator William Borah, the commission's original champion, expressed his disappointment. "If no constructive program is to result, if no statute is to be enacted or no legislation and control to be had, I myself do not care to have any interest in it." John L. Lewis dismissed it with little more than a smirk.

※ ※ ※

Governor Len Small was reelected in 1924 by a large margin, helped by the endorsement of the Illinois Federation of Labor. At the end of his second term the state of Illinois paid for the publication of a book naming Small as the author called *Illinois. Progress, 1921–1928*. The perversely wonderful book is a tribute to Small that few Roman emperors ever enjoyed, while, of course, omitting any hint of the corruption allegations. Lavishly illustrated with photos of avian tuberculosis inspection, before and after shots of highway construction, shoe repair classes for the "feebleminded" in state institutions and many other glimpses into the decade the book highlights the routine achievements of the executive branch departments.

In the chapter on the military and navy department, Brig. Gen. Carlos E. Black still in command, the strength of the national guard was measured by a long list of inventory including 29,971 pairs of "breeches, service, cotton," 16,777 pairs of "breeches, service, wool," 208 machine guns, nine airplanes and 120 horses to pull ambulances and wagons. The mission of the troops to ensure public safety at something called the Eucharistic Congress in Mundelein was celebrated. "This immense gathering of people was so well managed and handled that there was no accident or injury of any kind. The objective was accomplished by the preservation of peace and good order of society and by preventing violations of the laws of the road." The book also states in passing that "on several occasions, it was deemed necessary to send troops into Williamson County," the only mention of the only events still remembered from Gov. Small's administration.

Earlier the *Chicago Journal of Commerce* put his legacy in a true perspective. "No matter where an Illinoisan travels elsewhere in the country, if politics is mentioned, he is asked about Small. Small is one of the state's two burning disgraces of recent years. The other is the Herrin massacre." Before leaving office, Small paid the state $650,000 to settle a civil suit

10. Aftermath

connected with his diversion of public funds while he was state treasurer into a bank controlled by a state senator. The repayment bought him immunity from prosecution and secured his place as the most corrupt elected official in the most corrupt state.

After a lifetime of poor health habits and a difficult trip to the Alaska territory and the west coast, President Warren Harding died of heart failure in San Francisco on August 2, 1923. He was 57. The public was devastated. An estimated nine million people lined the tracks to witness the funeral train that took him back to Marion, Ohio. Only after he died did the corruption of his administration come to light. The rumors also began that his wife Florence poisoned him because of his philandering. With his death, the popularity Harding achieved during his life also died. He is often cited, along with James Buchanan and now Donald Trump, as among the worst presidents in American history. Calvin Coolidge, Harding's vice president, was visiting his family's rustic home in Vermont when a messenger reached him with the news. At 2:47 a.m., Coolidge was sworn in by the light of a kerosene lamp by his father, a notary public. His first act as president was to go back to bed.

Edward Brundage was scheduled to testify in a mob trial when on the morning of January 20, 1934, he dressed for work and, while his chauffer waited outside, went to the basement and shot himself in the chest.

Dee Hartwell continued serving as a circuit judge along with starting a law practice with John Hay. Hartwell died in 1933 at age 54. His widow married John Hay and they lived in Hartwell's house.

Delos Duty never ran for office again after being defeated by the Klan's candidate and being shot and wounded in his arms, legs and neck by drive by shooters. After leaving office he took a long rest in Arizona. He returned to Marion and started a private law practice. Twice married and divorced with two daughters, Duty lived alone most of his life. A 1961 near fatal traffic accident forced him to retire. Four years later he died at age 83. His body was cremated, and the ashes placed among other family members.

William Lester went on to operate a strip mine in Kentucky which failed and a bauxite mine in Arkansas, also a failure. He opened engineering consulting firms in Little Rock and Indianapolis before being stricken with paralysis in 1934. He was moved to his wife's family home in Augusta, Georgia, where he died in January 1935.

After Patrick O'Rourke testified before the Illinois House Committee, he disappeared from the public records. Presumably he returned to

The Herrin Massacre of 1922

Chicago but no one knows. Did he retell his story to strangers in a bar opening his collar for dramatic effect? Did he hide his part in history and try to resume a normal life? Did he return to Ireland? This part of the story is lost forever. He did, however, receive the considerable sum of $9,000 in a settlement against the UMWA.

Hugh Willis outlived his acquittal by ten years. He left the area and worked as an insurance salesman in Chicago. His body was returned to Herrin where he is buried in the city cemetery.

Of all of those associated with the massacre no one paid a larger or more lingering price than John L. Lewis. After he settled the strike he proceeded with his campaign for workers. He was simultaneously the most hated and best loved man in America. According to one of his biographers Lewis was the first labor leader to be considered a potential candidate for president of the United States. A typical miner's home had three pictures hanging on the wall: Jesus Christ, Franklin Roosevelt and John L. Lewis, not necessarily in that order. He was hated for taking the miners out on strike during World War II when American industry was desperately turning out the full scale production of tanks, airplanes, ships and a full array of weapons, and loved by coal mining families who credited him with improving their lives with money, safety and a kind of dignity found nowhere else in their lives. Lewis won the war against Frank Farrington in 1926 when Lewis exposed Farrington's $25,000 a year contract to work as a labor advisor for Peabody Coal while still serving as state president. Farrington was expelled from the union permanently.

Lewis was key in the creation of the Committee (later Congress) of Industrial Organizations or CIO, unions for workers without a particular skill or craft like the carpenters, electricians, plumbers and others who made up the America Federation of Labor or AFL. The merger of the two into the AFL-CIO was the high-water mark of American organized labor. Throughout his life Lewis battled the government, the right- and left-wing extremists, the combined forces of the employers and members of his own union, some of whom broke off into rival unions. During his battles the Herrin Massacre and the telegram he sent were always waiting in the shadows, waiting for another to pick up and bludgeon him. Even his most admiring biographer had a hard time dealing with his role in the massacre. "It was a very primitive murder, not as neat, as say, the executions of women in New York State's electric chair, where everything is arranged and done on schedule, with paid observers. But it was done just as finally.

10. Aftermath

Coal mining, like starving to death, is a primitive business," wrote Cecil Carnes in his 1936 book *John L. Lewis: Leader of Labor*.

Lewis was equally hated by the far left. In a 1937 the Socialist Labor Party attacked Lewis as a tool of capitalists constantly betraying the interests of the union members and the entire working class. In the booklet "John L. Lewis Exposed" Eric Hass writing about the events of 1922 said "thirty miners were massacred and twenty others wounded" in Herrin before Lewis capitulated to the mine operators. He claimed Lewis used the union miners to break the strike of 75,000 unorganized miners. "Lewis's cap-in-hand, obsequious biographer, Cecil Carnes, explained," Hass wrote, "'He could not, as a business unionist, risk a good contract by insisting upon too much.'"

On May 31, 1959, 80-year-old Lewis appeared on the television news program "Meet the Press." Defiant and articulate as ever, Lewis faced four journalists, including May Craig, a pioneer for women in the media, a frontline correspondent in World War II and then a columnist for the Portland, Maine, *Press Herald*. Craig asked Lewis if he was shocked by recent allegations of violence in the labor movement exposed by a Senate committee. "No more than I was shocked yesterday or the day before," her replied. Craig challenged him to accept responsibility for the morality of individuals' actions. "As a leader of labor, or one of its spokesmen, I'm not responsible for the morality of any part of our population," Lewis said. "You're getting into the area where the moral code is involved and the question of sin, wholesale or in the individual sense. The hunting down of sin and morality, and its eradication was not an enterprise within the purview or province of labor unions." Public outrage at labor unions was a "papier mache revolution," he said. Herrin was not even hinted but its legacy filled the screen.[8]

Lewis continued as president of the UMWA until his retirement in 1960, finishing 40 years leading the union. Before he died in 1969 he continued to influence the leadership, hand picking Tony Boyle as president in 1963. Lewis was buried in a simple grave in Oakridge Cemetery in Springfield, Illinois, not far from Abraham Lincoln's Tomb. After his death the union went through a tumultuous and violent period. Reformer Joseph Yabolanski ran against Boyle in 1969 and defeated him. Yabolanski along with his wife and daughter were murdered in their home by three men hired by Boyle. Following Boyle's conviction and imprisonment, the union purged itself of the violence and corruption and became as it is today an honest union, a strong voice in organized labor for working people despite its lower membership. Its former president Dick Trumka presently leads the AFL-CIO. The challenges faced by Trumka and other leaders have evolved as well. Recently, Delta Air Lines mounted a print and social media campaign aimed at its employees, advocating that union dues of about $700 a year could be put to better use: "A new video game system with the latest hits sounds like fun. Put your money towards that instead of paying dues to the union."

Epilogue: Herrin Today

Coal has been both a blessing and a curse to Herrin and southern Illinois. Nobody loved it but nobody wanted it to leave. Coal is leaving the region, leaving behind the scars on the land and on the bodies and souls of the people. Just before the 1922 strike, a high school principal in Johnson City did his own study and concluded that Illinois coal would last another 800 years, which was reported by a local newspaper.

He was wrong. Only about 4,000 people still work as miners in Illinois, and the number is dropping steadily. There is only one operating mine left in Williamson County, the Pond Creek mine owned by Williamson Energy, LLC. Miners in Williamson County today most often refer to the area's successful minor league baseball team. Unemployment in Williamson County exceeds the national and state levels.

Coal may be leaving the United States, not because of environmental activism, which has succeeded in identifying it as a key factor in global warming, but because of Wall Street.[1] The Coal Index, the leading gauge of the industry, has moved steadily downward in recent years. Falling coal prices have decimated the industry, resulting in a 94 percent drop in value from $68 billion to $4 billion in a five-year period. Coal companies began falling like dominos, Patriot Coal, Walter Energy, James River Coal and Alpha Natural Resources filing bankruptcy until Arch Coal, the second largest coal company in America followed in 2016, as did the largest coal company Peabody Energy soon afterwards. In 2015, coal production fell nationally to 900 million tons from 1 billion tons the previous year. Although much coal is still used in power generation, companies are switching to natural gas to run the turbines. In fact, it was widely predicted natural gas fueled generation would exceed coal-based generation by 2016. Coal exports fell 20 percent in 2015. President Obama's decision to stop issuing permits to mine on federal land, a long-sought goal of environmentalists, had little

Epilogue: Herrin Today

effect when no investors are willing to literally sink their money into a coal mine.

In 2016, Oregon mandated the elimination of coal fueled power production by 2035. Hawaii had already set its eyes on a total ban by 2045. Vermont has restricted coal usage to seventy five percent by 2032, and giant power consuming states California and New York both have enacted 50 percent restrictions by 2030. Other states are certain to follow. With the Impending end of coal mining there are new sets of problems for the broken people and broken land left behind. There are programs in place to retrain coal miners for new jobs, including in renewable energy fields, but they pay far less than the mines did. Wyoming has mandated computer science courses in K to 12 to prepare the next generation for a post coal economy. Underground mines closed and forgotten about for decades are causing new problems on the surface as the mines collapse. Houses and public buildings across Illinois have been experiencing damages caused by mine subsidence, a problem that will continue until the last tunnel is reclaimed by the earth. A brand-new school in Benld, Illinois, was split in two parts as cracks spread across the floors and walls. It may just be a small down payment for the government and taxpayers. Permits to operate coal mines were tied to the promise to self-bond the cleanup costs after the mine closed. With the increasing pace of bankruptcies, the promises are disappearing. leaving the public to pay for the reclamation. More than $3.3 billion in self-bonding is in danger of disappearing in bankruptcy courts. Not all of that will fall on the taxpayers but more than enough will

The end of coal mining has become a reality in the land of its birth. In 2015, the last operating deep pit mine in England in the village of Kellingly closed its gates forever, and in 2016 Scotland closed its last coal burning plant Longannet in Fife.[2] What coal the United Kingdom needs for it power plants will be imported until as the government plans, the last coal fired power plant will close. More than coal mining ended in Kellingly; it was the end of a chapter in labor history often marked by strikes and unrest, the end of a symbol of a culture so often and often inaccurately played on stage and screen, and on the pages of books written by outsiders. The British coal miner, with his face covered in the stereotype black coal dust and the pickaxe resting on his shoulder, along with his long-suffering family above ground, was a noble figure. But the hard, dangerous realities of mining, the life shortening brutal conditions are not worth the nostalgia. It is a lesson for America if, as may happen, coal mining eventually comes to end here. Herrin is a textbook for that lesson. The story is mixed in other parts of the world. China put a freeze on new coal mines in 2015 and the following year halted the planned construction of 250 coal powered plants, although it will continue to generate electricity from the existing plants for the foreseeable future. India and southeast Asia are actually projected to burn more coal in their push for development. But the global outlook for coal is bleak for miners, while bright for environmentalists.

Some in Southern Illinois still cling to their identity as part of "coal country." They react to any critical look at coal mining as "coal bashing," a charge leveled against the author after a university press at the last moment canceled publication this book under pressure from a coal lobbyist. The self-delusion of coal country is hard to maintain given the facts. In 2019 Vista Energy announced the closing of four coal-fired power plants in Illinois. In the neighboring state of Kentucky, where there are no longer any union miners, the Blackjewel LLC coal company, a subsidiary of Revelation Energy, suddenly declared Chapter 11 bankruptcy. About three hundred miners in Kentucky along with another 1,800 employees around the nation either did not receive paychecks or were issued rubber checks that bounced for insufficient funds. Blackjewel, along with every mine in Kentucky, violated state law requiring coal companies to buy performance bonds to cover wages. The *Lexington Herald Leader* newspaper found that none of the companies had complied with the law for the previous five years, The unemployed miners and their supporters set up a round the clock blockade and encampment complete with a children's playroom on the track leading out of the Cumberland, Kentucky, mine to prevent the shipment of about $1,000,000 worth of coal. The protestors finally had to leave to find some other way to survive. Other miners and their families are protesting the shortfall of funding for black lung victims just as the deadly disease is increasing among the dwindling number of miners. These are facts. Calling them "coal bashing" will not change them.

Just as Southern Illinois has not come to terms with the bleak future of coal, Herrin and Williamson County have never come to terms with their past. All official public records of the investigations and trials once in the county courthouse are "lost," but to be fair, they were probably "lost" long before anyone working in the courthouse today was born. To celebrate Williamson County's sesquicentennial in 1989 the Southern Illinoisan newspaper published a special souvenir edition of 80 pages of stories and congratulatory advertisements including a form letter from President George H.W. Bush which spoke of the "deep sense of community, of responsibility towards one's neighbor and the common good." On

Epilogue: Herrin Today

page 78, far away from the stories of the glorious pioneers, there was a short article on the massacre. Missing from the article was any mention of the cheering crowds, the display and discretion of the dead, or just about anything that could embarrass or upset the readers during the 150th celebration.[3]

The Norge plant was operating in Herrin in 1989 and the special section cited it as an example of how Herrin was expanding its economy away from the failing coal industry. The plant was sold to Maytag which expanded the production lines until it reached the high water mark of 2,000 employees in 2003.Two year later Whirlpool bought Maytag and began downsizing the Herrin plant, sending jobs to Mexico, until the doors were shut forever at the end of 2006. Other smaller facilities are still operating but the blow of losing the plant hit Herrin and its people hard. Recently a small company bought the closed Maytag plant for $1 million with plans to update it for small scale operations. Recent news that Swanson would open a small plant was welcome. A regional economic development commission runs an aggressive campaign to attract business but does not mention coal mining.

Driving into Herrin today, you pass the almost the mandatory Walmart, McDonald's, Pizza Hut, Taco Bell, the Kroger grocery store, bowling alleys, car dealerships and the other fixture of small town America in the 21st century. Downtown, as in many other small towns in America, has been decimated by Wal-Mart yet a few small businesses carry on. Herrin once had nine theaters, including two drive-ins. All are gone now but one old cinema has been remodeled.

"Herrinites take pride in the community's history. This is displayed on holidays when American flags adorn Park Avenue, when the townspeople watch a homecoming parade and when veterans have special ceremonies: around the Doughboy Memorial—a symbol of freedom and remembrance of those who fought for our land," according to the unofficial promotional web page Town Square Publications.com. The 2016 website of the Herrin Area Historical Society in its history of Herrin has not one word about the massacre, the gang wars or any other incidents of violence. It does claim for Herrin the nickname the Gateway City marking Herrin "as the gateway to opportunity." Recently a 1914 White truck appeared on EBay as the "Scab Killing" truck used by miners. "Yes, here's chance to reminisce about the Good Old Days with your buddies at the car show, as you show then where the miners hooked up the chains used to drag the men to their deaths." The seller admitted there was no documentation for the claim,

Epilogue: Herrin Today

which in any event was contradicted by the facts. There is a memorial to the coal mining heritage of Herrin, a statue of presumably a father and son, the father ready to go to work in a mine with a hard hat with an acetylene lamp and a lunch pail in one hand, the other grabbing the upstretched arm of a boy carrying a school book with his other hand presumably to get an education that will keep him out of the mines forever. It captures the universal sacrifice parents make for their children—an aspiration not always fulfilled.

Other history minded residents have marked the "Charlie Birger Fun Trail" and one Charlie Birger impersonator makes a living giving presentations.[4] The old Franklin County jail in Benton has built a replica of the gallows used to hang Birger and paranormal groups routinely visit the old jail to investigate and to receive messages from Charlie's ghost which supposedly haunts the cells.

Herrin stayed out of the national spotlight for the most part until 2016. A transgender girl scout selling cookies was turned away by an angry neighbor who told her "nobody wants to buy cookies from a boy in a dress." Supporters from all parts of the country rallied around her, helping her sell more than three thousand boxes of cookies.

But it is harder to remember or celebrate the massacre. It's hard to approach a friendly resident of Herrin or environs and ask about their grandfathers and fathers, who were criminally liable for murdering more people than Charles Manson, more than Jeffery Dahmer, more than Richard Speck. Does it put it in a more positive perspective that the mob, on June 21–22, fell short of Ted Bundy's or John Wayne Gacy's records? How can an innocent person deal with their legacy other than to forget or deny it? How can the good people of today's Herrin or Germany or Japan live with the knowledge of what their families once did? Some people may see Charlie Birger's ghost haunting the present. Where are the ghosts of Herrin? Where are the ghosts of Otis Clark, Hugh Willis, Melvin Thaxton or Delos Duty? And what of the victims?

More than a thousand rains and snowfalls have long since washed the blood away, literally and figuratively. Herrin and its people today are innocent. Anyone who had even the slightest connection to the massacre has long since died. Many of those who committed the murders or witnessed them lie dead in the same cemetery where the worst killings took place. Walk down the well-maintained rows of headstones and look at the dates. Did this person slash the throat of one of the victims? Did this man tie his hands? Did the woman lying in the grave next to him cheer along

Epilogue: Herrin Today

with others, many of whom are also buried there? Did this woman who was seven years old in 1922 watch her uncle kill people in front of her eyes? Did she join other children and their parents to mock and degrade the dead bodies put on display? The earth that covers them and grass and trees growing over them have left the questions forever unanswered. The scars the Lester mine left on the land are healing, bandaged by a thick growth of green which could if left undisturbed for another million years or so lay down another thin seam of coal for others to mine. But if the dead and the land could speak what would they say? And who of us would be willing to listen and learn?

The unclaimed and unrecovered dead of the massacre lay for decades in unmarked, unknown, unremembered and unvisited graves. In the early 21st century, a heroic four-year effort using cutting edge technology, including ground penetrating radar, uncovered and identified what are very likely the victims of the massacre. Some of the plots where they were laid were illegally sold to the families of other decedents which were buried on top of massacre victims.[5] Nearby in the cemetery the people of Herrin recently erected a tombstone-like monument with the names of seventeen of the victims carved into the surface. On the other side of the stone is a dedication to "the men who lost their lives in the conflict of June 21 & 22, 1922, a time of labor unrest and lawlessness which still stands as the largest loss of life due to a labor dispute in the country a tragedy known as the Herrin Massacre." The $2,600 stone was financed by private donors in the area. At the dedication Herrin Mayor Steve Frattini said the stone "is going to bring us closer to closure of that era and situation."[6]

However well intentioned, the memorial will not bring closure. The forces within the human soul which were on full display that long-ago summer are still there, waiting to erupt.

No one alive today was either a perpetrator or victim of the massacre. No living person owes the dead an apology or remedy, whether real or symbolic. The decedents of the mob in Herrin are not responsible for anything that happened that June day. Any apology, however heartfelt, would be a meaningless, hollow gesture. The ritualistic public apologies for events of the past from people who bear absolutely no responsibility for them to people who never actually suffered whether for slavery, the genocide of Native Americans, the many acts of discrimination and injustice that stud American history are pointless exercises. Herrin does not need to apologize but it does need to remember for its own sake if no one else's. For decades the living in Herrin both forgot and hid their history.

Epilogue: Herrin Today

The stone monument is not as much an honor to the dead but a charge to the future to atone for nearly a century of silence.

There are open spots in the cemetery where some of the victims remain buried, joined nearby by other paupers. Standing on the space in the Herrin cemetery, amid the plastic flowers decorating the more fortunate headstones, amid the sound of cars passing by on the road one can turn towards every compass point and see the woods fringing the land in almost every direction, near or far. But with the eyes of history one can imagine seeing beyond the horizon to faraway lands and times like Auschwitz, the gulags of the Soviet Union, the killing fields of Cambodia, Tiananmen Square, Rwanda, Paris, Brussels, Jonestown and the village of My Lai in Vietnam, and places closer to Herrin: Columbine, Sandy Hook, Virginia Tech, Oklahoma City, Littleton, Ft. Hood, San Bernardino, lower Manhattan, Orlando, Las Vegas, Sutherland Springs, Parkland, Santa Fe, Pittsburgh, Thousand Oaks, Virginia Beach, El Paso, Dayton, Odessa and Jersey City. Surrounding this bare ground all over the planet there is a veritable constellation of massacres, mass murders, acts of terrorism and war. But here the victims of the Herrin Massacre rest, spared any further injury from that day in June of 1922 and safe from the horrors and deaths that stretched before them in the century and centuries ahead.

Chapter Notes

Introduction

The Oldham Paisley Scrapbooks (OPS) are published in three volumes, Vol. 1, "Before & After the Riot," a combined Vol. 1-A and 1-B, sharing the title "Riot," with no apparent division between the two, and a combined Vols. 2, "First Trial," and 3, "Second Trial," again with no apparent division. To avoid confusion the three will be cited as Vol. 1, Vol. 1-A and Vol. 2. Also, some pages are stamped with numbers, some have handwritten page numbers and some have no page numbers at all. To make things worse, the numbers are often in no logical order; for example, the first few pages of one volume are numbered in the hundreds. Further, the entries are not always in chronological order. Some pages are repeated. Despite these problems the scrapbooks are a vital source.

1. "Coal may be leaving," Associated Press reports.
2. "recent study," *The Guardian*, March 25, 2019.
3. "Nineteen coal-fired plants," *Washington Post*, April 2, 2019.
4. "Kentucky Coal Museum," Louisville *Courier Journal*, April 7, 2017.

Chapter 1

1. "John Hoover," Ackerman, *Young J. Edgar*.
2. "In the midst of the conflict," from biographies of John L. Lewis.
3. "We mined the coal," Hass, *John L. Lewis Exposed*, 21.
4. "not only unjustified," Ackerman, *Young J. Edgar*, 100.
5. "cities in darkness," *ibid*.
6. "ran against Gompers," Dubofsky, *John L. Lewis*, 42.
7. "The only thing," Harding letter to Frank Scobey, Dec. 30, 1919.
8. "dogs barking": The full text reads: "He writes the worst English that I have ever encountered. It reminds me of a string of wet sponges; it reminds me of tattered washing on the line; it reminds me of stale bean soup, of college yells, of dogs barking idiotically through endless nights. It is so bad that a sort of grandeur creeps into it. It drags itself out of the dark abysm of pish, and crawls insanely up the topmost pinnacle of posh. It is rumble and bumble. It is flap and doodle. It is balder and dash."
9. "McAdoo," Dean, *Warren G. Harding*, 72.
10. "He was about as handsome," Angle, *Bloody Williamson*, 511.
11. "If there is anythin wrong," Sullivan, *Our Times: The Twenties*, 242. For more on Harding see "This Presidential Speech on Race Shocked a Nation in 1921," by Greg Bailey, Oct. 26, 2016, available online at http://narrative.ly/this-presidential-speech-on-race-shocked-the-nation-in-1921/.
12. "heard men in Congress," Ronald Radosh, and Allis Radoshaug, "Rethinking Warren G. Harding," *Slate*, Aug. 27, 2015.

Chapter Notes

Chapter 2

Unless otherwise noted, the main source for this chapter is *Williamson County Illinois in the World War* by Hal W. Trovillion (Williamson County War History Society, 1919), available online at https://archive.org/details/williamsoncounty00bair.

1. "Herrin had the mixed blessing," Malcolm and Webb, *Seven Stranded Coal Towns*, 3.
2. "The tangled and complex story": There are several good books on the Bloody Vendetta, including *Bloody Williamson* by Paul Angle, and *The Bloody Vendetta of Southern Illinois* by Milo Erwin and Jon Musgrove.
3. "Sam T. Brush," "Troops Against Strikers," *New York Times*, July 1, 1899; Historic Souvenir of Williamson County Illinois, 185–187; "White Men Kill Negroes," *New York Times*, Sept. 17, 1899; "Governor Says Negroes Must Stop" *New York Times*, Sept. 18, 1899.

Chapter 3

1. "Less than one percent," A Compilation of the Reports of the Mining Industry of Illinois from the Earliest Records to 1954.
2. "Two Bucyrus steam shovels": The full list of equipment at the Lester mine is in *A Caterwaul from Egypt* by Woodrow W, Everett, Jr.; also listed in OPS, Vol. 1, unnumbered page.
3. "Alex Howart," Wikipedia "Amazon Army," "Amazon Army Remembered," *Topeka Capitol-Journal*, Dec. 9, 2001; "Amazon Army Protested Unfair Labor," *Wichita Eagle*, Oct. 4, 2010.
4. "Alex Howart," Wikipedia.
5. "I have known Alex Howat," Wikipedia.
6. "They said that he was scabby," *The American Flint*, March 1922, 40.

Chapter 4

1. "I did not intend," E.H. Renaud's testimony in the Coroner inquest.
2. "Addressing her as," OPS, Vol. 2., handwritten page number 196.
3. "We came down here," Angle, *Bloody Williamson*, 15.
4. "What the Goddamned hell," Angle, *Bloody Williamson*, 14.
5. "Pulling him out," *ibid*.
6. "I eats them alive," OPS, Vol. 2, handwritten page number 189.
7. "Another group," OPS, Vol. 2, handwritten page number 192.
8. "A group of three friends," OPS, Vol. 2, handwritten page number 195.
9. "W.M. Burton," Parker, *The Herrin Massacre*, 92–93.
10. "Crystal radio," "Looking the Other Way: A Study of the Local Press Coverage of the Events Surrounding the Herrin Massacre of June 22, 1922," by Jim R. Martin, unpublished dissertation, 1993, 63.
11. "You and the State's Attorney," Angle, *Bloody Williamson*, 14.
12. "We know our business," OPS, Vol. 2, handwritten page number 193.
13. "Lay down on that damn sheriff," OPS, Vol. 1-A, unnumbered page.
14. "Indianapolis": The text of Lewis' telegram was widely reprinted.

Chapter 5

1. "If it takes all summer," *New York Times*, June 22, 1922. The well-known original statement was made by Gen. Ulysses S Grant: "I propose to fight it out on this line if it takes all summer."
2. "Charge it to the union," Parker, *The Herrin Massacre*, 27.
3. "We don't want any trouble," Parker, *The Herrin Massacre*, 94.
4. "Otis Alexander," Parker, *The Herrin Massacre*, 93.

Chapter 6

In general, the story of the events of June 22 comes from witnesses statements during the trials and the investigation; but also from the Illinois House of Representatives investigation, contemporary newspaper stories, and to a limited extent personal recollections of witnesses.

1. "Perhaps one or more": This is speculation. Nobody knows for certain if anyone attempted or succeeded in escaping but it was a question people asked at the time. See the *Harrisburg Daily Register*, June 26, 2012.
2. "Robert Officer," *New York Times*, Dec. 29, 1922.
3. "Some of whom had recently served": Lists of returning veterans of the war ran in Trovillian's *Williamson County Illinois in the World War*.
4. "Bernard Jones," testimony of Jones.
5. "Articles of war," OPS, Vol. 1-A, unnumbered page.
6. "See these white sons of bitches," OPS, Vol. 1-A, 7.
7. "Anybody got a shell?" OPS, Vol. 1-A, 8.
8. "They're hard to kill" ... OPS, Vol. 1-A, 51.
9. "Harold Graves," Graves, *We Remember*, self-published, nd, 6.

Chapter 7

At the time there were accusations that other strikebreakers were killed and their bodies dumped in ponds. Apparently, there was some effort to search for those bodies but none were found or at least none were reported to be found. The evidence for these claims of additional victims does not, in the author's judgment, support the claims. Whatever efforts were put into a search for additional victims quickly dissipated. The truth is, that like other aspects of the Herrin Massacre, no one knows for certain nor can anyone ever know. Beliefs and rumors, however heartfelt and however expressed, are not evidence. Associated Press report June 29, 1922.

1. "Mrs. Eubans," OPS, Vol. 1-A, unnumbered page.
2. "Richard Battle," *Manufacturers' Record*, August 24, 1922.
3. "Huns, bohunks and wops," *Mining and Metallurgy*, July, 1922, 5.
4. "Lester," *The World*, June 24, 1922; *St. Louis Post-Dispatch*, June 23, 1922.
5. "Like a family quarrel," *New York Times*, July 31, 1922.
6. "Fred Macy," *Ogden Standard-Examiner*, June 28, 1922.
7. "Also moving north," Boaz, *The Cry Room and Other Places*.
8. "Don't believe all you hear," OPS, Vol. 1, unnumbered page.
9. "McGowan," Trovillian, *Williamson County Illinois in the World War*.
10. "McGowan and the jurors," Parker, *The Herrin Massacre*, 46–49. The report was published widely.
11. "The Goddamn operators," Nial, *The Twenties in America; Politics and History*, 60.
12. "Myers," Congressional Record, June 24, 1922.
13. "Four days later," Congressional Record, June 28, 1922.
14. "Lewis," *United Mine Workers Journal*, July 1, 1922.
15. "Hughes," Letter from Secretary of State Charles Evan Hughes to Gov. Len Small, August 4, 1922, with enclosure from the embassy of Mexico; also *New York Times*, Aug. 8, 1922.
16. "Camlin," *New York Times*, Aug. 22, 1922.
17. "Railroad Labor Act," Russel, *The Shadow of Blooming Grove*, 547.
18. "joint session," *New York Tribune*, Aug. 19, 1922.
19. "Canton," Daugherty and Dixon, *The Inside Story of the Harding Tragedy*.
20. "William Allen White," *New York Tribune*, Dec. 31, 1922.

Chapter 8

1. "Do Not Fear Punishment," *Urbana Daily Courier*, June 23, 1922.
2. "Harding," *New York Tribune*, Aug. 19, 1922.
3. "National Coal Association," *New York Times*, July 31, 1922.
4. "Hartwell," Trovillian, *Williamson County Illinois in the World War*, 283.

Chapter Notes

5. "Brundage," *Illinois Blue Book*, 1922, 28.
6. "The fear has touched," OPS, Vol. 1-A, 56.
7. "All the earmarks," OPS, Vol. 1, 35; *The Nation*, Oct. 11, 1922, 357.
8. "The atrocities and cruelties," OPS. Vol. l, 33, 34.
9. "Had faithfully," *The Outlook*, Oct. 14, 1922, 174.
10. "Arraignment," OPS. Vol. 1, 41.
11. "treated to meals," OPS, Vol. 1, 44; OPS Vol. 1-A, 71.
12. "There will be perfect order," OPS, Vol. 2, unnumbered page.
13. "Opening argument": ,The full text of Kerr's opening argument was reprinted in the booklet "The Other Side of Herrin" published by The Illinois Mine Workers, undated but probably 1923.
14. "Bert Grace," OPS, Vol. 2, handwritten page number 176.
15. "William Goodman," OPS, Vol. 2, handwritten page number 175.
16. "P.J. O'Rourke," *Chicago Tribune*, Dec. 21, 1922; OPS, Vol. 1-A, handwritten page numbered 182.
17. "Bernard Jones." *Ibid*.
18. "William Cairns," *Ibid*.
19. "Otis Clark," *Chicago Tribune*, Jan. 20, 1923.
20. "Farrington," *Marion Semi-Weekly Leader*, Nov. 10, 1922.
21. "Legislative branch," The Journal of House of Representatives, June 30, 1923.
22. "Will Warder," *Ibid.*, 1448.
23. "Angrily noted," *Ibid.*, 1462.
24. "In a wasteful and extravagant manner," *Chicago Tribune*, July 1, 1923.
25. Following the trials there were accusations of jurors receiving bribes. There was never any substantial evidence to support these claims so the author in his judgment declines to present them in the chapter.
26. "Col. Hunter, despite," *Chicago Tribune*, Oct. 8, 1923.

Chapter 9

1. "One of the more unusual," Harper, "Civilization of Herrin, Illinois," *Tuscaloosa News*, Oct. 10, 1924.
2. "I didn't follow," oral history interview with Paul Cadmus, 1988 Mar 22–May 5, Archives of American Art, Smithsonian Institution.
3. A color copy of the painting is online at https://www.vulture.com/2019/03/the-painting-jerrry-saltz-cant-stop-thinking-about.html.
4. "Lynching was more than hanging": See also "Lynching in America: Confronting the Legacy of Racist Terror," published by the Equal Justice Initiative, 2nd ed., 2015, for an excellent examination of the history of lynching.
5. "A bizarre footnote," *The Crisis*, Vol. 24, No. 6 , Oct. 1922, 265 and other pages.
6. "Senator Harris," *New York Times*, July 14, 1922.
7. "Senator William Shields," *Ibid.*
8. "Center, Texas," *Manufacturers' Record*, July 27, 1922, 56.
9. "Good negroes," *New York Times*, Dec. 2, 1922.
10. "In September 1923," *New York Times*, Sept. 10, 1923; *Time*, Sept. 24, 1923.
11. "It was even too much," *New York Times*, Sept. 16, 1923.
12. "We are not Communists," *Time*, Sept. 24, 1923.
13. "Dear Comrade," letter of Feb. 17, 1923.
14. "James P. Cannon, Nov. 27, 1922.
15. "Bolsheviki!" Coleman, *Man and Coal*, 122.
16. "The Society wrote Lewis," undated letter.
17. "In a letter to one of its members," letter of July 31, 1922, to Charles Stewart Davison.
18. "Even the mainstream American Legion," *The American Legion Weekly*, July 21, 1922.
19. "It is necessary," Address of the Attorney General of the United States, Canton, Ohio, Oct. 21, 1923, published as a booklet now available online.
20. "Another unique view," "The Herrin Massacre," An address delivered before the Association of Life Insurance Counsel, May 24, 1923, at Milwaukee, WI, by Follet W. Bull, General Counsel, Security Life Insurance Company of America, Chicago, recorded on microfilm in the New York City Public Library.

Chapter Notes

21. "Lytton," *Chicago Tribune*, June 25, 1922.
22. "Decided the case," *United Mine Workers v. Coronado Coal Co.*, 259 U.S. 344 (1922) http://www.kevincmurphy.com/uatw-legacies-labor.html.
23. "It ran a letter from," *The Open Shop Review*. The letter, dated June 24, 1922, refers to an editorial of the same date, an obvious mistake on one or both of the dates.
24. "Three weeks after... *Manufacturers' Record*, July 13, 1922.
25. "Hoffman," *Chicago Tribune*, June 26, 1922.
26. "Coolidge," Dubofsky, *John L. Lewis*, 85.
27. "But not every effort," *Chicago Tribune*, June 28, 1938.

Chapter 10

1. "Boswell," *Daily Register*, June 22, 2012.
2. "Modern history," Trovillian, *Persuading God Back to Herrin*.
3. "Otis Clark," Foster, *Victims of the Herrin Massacre*, 88–89.
4. "These boys": Excerpts of Darrow's closing argument are online at http://famous-trials.com/leopoldandloeb/2339-summations.
5. "Herrin, until lately obscure," *The Outlook*, Aug. 9, 1922.
6. "Arthur Rothstein": The photographs are online at https://www.loc.gov/search/?fa=subject%3Aherrin..
7. Bituminous Operators Special Committee, May 16, 1923. The full 50-page report is available online.
8. "Meet the Press," May 31, 1959, https://www.youtube.com/watch?v=jILdBf2Hgsc.

Epilogue

1. "Coal may be leaving," Associated Press reports.
2. "Deep pit mine in England," BBC.
3. "Sesquicentennial," Happy 150th! special edition of *The Southern Illinoisan*, May 14, 1989.
4. "Charlie Burger," "The Bootlegger Who Took Down the KKK," *Riverfront Times*, March 23, 2015.
5. "In the early 21st century," *The Southern Illinoisan*, Nov. 15, 2013. The full story of the search for the missing bodies is the subject of *Herrin Massacre* by Scott Doody.
6. "Recently erected," *The Southern Illinoisan*, June 1, 2015; Associated Press, June 20, 2015.

Bibliography

Ackerman, Kenneth D. *Young J. Edgar: The Red Scare, 1919–1920*. New York: Carroll & Graf, 2007.
The American Reader. New York: Alfred A. Knopf 1958
Ameringer, Oscar. *If You Don't Weaken: The Autobiography of Oscar Ameringer*. New York: Holt, 1940.
Angle, Paul. *Bloody Williamson*. New York: Alfred A. knopf, 1952.
Anonymous, various writers for *Time* magazine. *Time Capsule/1923*. New York: Time Life Books, 1967.
Anonymous, various writers for the *Wall Street Journal. A History of Organized Felony and Folly*. New York: 1922.
Boaz, John. *The Cry Room and Other Places*. Victoria, BC, Canada: Trafford, 2004.
Brown, Malcolm, and John N. Webb. *Seven Stranded Coal Towns: A Study of an American Depressed Area*. Washington, D.C.: United States Government Printing Office, 1941.
Carnes, Cecil. *John L. Lewis: Leader of Labor*. New York: Robert Speller Publishing Corp., 1936.
Coleman, Alister. *Man and Coal*. New York: Farrar & Rinehart, 1943.
Daugherty, Harry M., and Thomas Dixon. *The Inside Story of the Harding Tragedy*. Reissued by Western Islands, Boston, MA, 1975. Originally published 1932.
Dean, John. *Warren G. Harding*. New York: Times Books, 2004.
DeNeal, Gary. *A Knight of Another Sort*, Carbondale, IL: Southern Illinois University Press, 1998.
Devine, Edward T. *Coal: Economic Problems of Mining, Marketing and Consumption of Anthracite and Soft Coal in the United States, Facts and Remedies*. Bloomimgton, IL: American Review Service Press, 1925.
Doody, Scott. *Herrin Massacre*. No location listed: Dick's Chicken Shack Productions, 2013.
Dubofsky, Melvin. *John L. Lewis*. New York: Quadrangle, 1977.
Everett Jr, Woodrow W. *A Caterwaul from Egypt*. New York: Vantage Press, 1970.
Federal Writers Project. *Illinois: A Descriptive and Historical Guide*.
Foster, John F. *Victims of the Herrin Massacre*. Self-published, 2015.
Galligan, George. *In Bloody Williamson*. Self-published, 1927.
Graves, Harold K. *We Remember: Reflections on Early Experiences in Herrin, Illinois*. Self-published, 1965.
Hallgren, Mauritz Alfred. *Seeds of Revolt*. New York: Knopf, 1937.
Hamilton, Walton H. "Problem of Bituminous Coal," New Haven, CT: Yale University Press, 1926.
Hass, Eric. *John L. Lewis Exposed*. Self-published, 1937.
Hill, E. Bishop. *Complete History of Southern Illinois' Gang War*. Self-published, date unknown (possibly 1927).

Bibliography

Hunt, Edward Eyre. *What the Coal Commission Found*. Baltimore, MD: Williamson & Willkins Co., 1925.
Illinois Coal Operators Association. *What Is Behind the Wage Contract with Illinois Miners?* Self published, probably 1922.
Illinois Department of Mines and Minerals. *A Compilation of the Reports of the Mining Industry of Illinois from the Earliest Records to 1954*. Springfield, IL, 1954.
The Illinois Mine Workers. *The Other Side of Herrin*. Self-published, probably 1923.
Kearns Goodwin, Doris. *Bully Pulpit*. New York: Simon & Schuster, 2013.
Kamp, Joseph P. *The Hell of Herrin Rages Again*. New Haven, CT: Constitutional Educational League, 1937.
Lauck, W. Jett. *The Trade Union as the Basis for Collective Bargaining*. Published by the United Mine Workers of America, 1920.
Lewis, John L. *The Miners' Fight for American Standards*. Indianapolis: Bell Publishers, 1925.
Lovestone, Jay. *The Government, Strikebreaker: A Study of the Role of the Government in the Recent Industrial Crisis*. Published by the Workers Party of America, 1923.
Martin, Jim R. *Looking the Other Way: A Study of the Coal Press Coverage of the Events Surrounding the Herrin Massacre of June 22, 1922*. Unpublished thesis, 1993.
Murphy, Kevin C. *Uphill All the Way: The Fortunes of Progressivism, 1919–1929*. Published online, 2013.
Murray, Richard K. *The Harding Era*. Newtown, CT: American Political Biography Press, 2000.
Myerscough, Tom. *The Name Is Lewis—John L*. Self-published, date unknown, likely early 1930s.
Paisley, Oldham. Scapbooks of period clippings, published in book format by the Williamson County Historical Society, Marion, IL.
Palmer, Nial A. *The Twenties in America; Politics and History*. Edinberg University Press, 2006.
Parker, Chatland, *The Herrin Massacre*. Self-published, 1923.
Ridings, Jim. *Len Small: Governors and Gangsters*. Herscher, IL: Sideshow Bosoks, 2009.
Russell, Francis. *The Shadow of Blooming Grove*. New York: McGraw-Hill, 1968.
Small, Len. *Illinois. Progress, 1921–1928*. Springfield, IL: Schnepp & Barnes, 1928.
Sullivan, Mark. *Our Times: The Twenties*. New York: Scribners, 1935.
Trovillion, Hal W. "Old Times in Herrin," *The Herrin News*, 1922.
_____. "Persuading God Back to Herrin," *The Herrin News*, 1925.
_____. *Williamson County Illinois in the World War*, Williamson County War History Society, 1919.
U.S. Department of Labor. *Handbook of American Trade-Unions: 1929 Edition*. Washington. D.C.: Government Printing Office
Wilcox, J.F., *Historical Souvenir of Williamson County, Illinois*. Effingham, IL: LeCrone Press, 1905.
Wright, Helen S. *Coal's Worst Year*. Boston. MA: Gorham Press, 1924.

Newspapers and Magazines

The American Flint
The American Legion Weekly
Boston Herald
Brooklyn Eagle
Carbondale Free Press
Chicago Tribune (also called the *Chicago Daily Tribune*)
Collier's
Daily Register (Harrisburg, IL)
Foreign Policy
Greater New York
The Guardian
Herrin News
The Huffington Post
Law and Labor
Lexington Herald Leader

Bibliography

Literary Digest
Louisville *Courier-Journal*
Manufacturers' *Record of America*
Marion Daily Republican
Marion Evening Post
Marion Semi-Weekly Leader
Mining and Metallurgy
The Nation
New York
New York Herald
New York Times
New York Tribune
The New York World
The New Yorker
The Open Shop Review
The Outlook
The Riverfront Times
St. Louis Globe Democrat
St. Louis Post Dispatch
St. Louis Star
Slate
The Southern Illinoisan
Springfield (MA) *Republican*
State Journal Register
Time
Topeka Capitol-Journal
Tuscaloosa News
United Mine Workers of America Journal
Urbana Daily Courier
Wall Street Journal
Washington Post
Wichita Eagle
Williamson County Miner

Digital and Electronic Media

BBC web page
MiningTechnology.com
NBC, *Meet the Press* PBS, "Newshour"

Index

Adams, Joe 136
Alexander, Otis 42, 44, 50
Allen, Henry J. 70
Amazon Army 30
American Civil Liberties Union (ACLU) 121
American Defense Society 122
American Federation of Labor 35
American Legion 123
Anderson. Robert 76
Aristotle 7

Baldwin, Roger 120
Belleville (IL) 116
Benld (IL) 3, 156
Bernard, Fred 47, 58, 70
Birger, Charlie 134, 136, 137, 153
Bituminous Operators Special Committee 141, 143
Black, Gen. Carlos 41, 42, 48, 108, 110, 144
Black, Dr. J.T. 61
Blair Mountain 14, 15, 49
Bloomberg, Michael 3
Bonnie and Clyde 133
Borah, William 80, 81, 141, 144
Boswell, Arlie O. 135
Boyle, Tony 147
Brooklyn (IL) 116
Brown, James 54, 56, 93, 104
Brown, W.J. 46
Brundage, Edward 68, 71, 81, 88, 89, 90, 91, 93, 94, 103, 106, 110, 145
Brush, Sam T. 21, 23, 32, 46
Brydon, John C. 120
Bull, Follett 73, 125–127
Bursum, Holm Olaf 81
Burton, W.J. 46

Cadmus, Paul 113–115
Cairns, William 30, 57, 100

Calder, William 118
Camlin, John 89
Capone, Al 133
Carnhagi, Joe 60, 94, 99, 101
Carter, Laban 21
Carterville (IL) 21, 23
Childers, Jesse 93
China 4, 7, 9
Churchill, Winston 2
Clark, Edward Young 134
Clark, Lizzy 55, 94
Clark, Otis 43, 48, 55, 56, 92, 93, 98, 99, 100, 101, 102, 103, 104, 105, 135, 136, 143, 153
coal 2–4, 7, 28
Coal Commission 41, 143, 144
Collinsville (IL) 116
Colp (IL) 105
Committee (later Congress) of Industrial Unions (CIO) 130, 146
Communists 121–122
Coolidge, Calvin 131, 145
coroner's report 74–75
Cox, David 16
Cox, George 94
Crenshaw, Ed 28
Crenshaw Crossing 47, 49, 55, 98, 107
Cronyn, Thoreau 73, 78

Darrow, Clarence 137
Daugherty, Harry 69, 85, 123
Davis, Altha 38, 101
Davis, Robert 41, 50
Debs, Eugene 17, 18
Drew, George 46
Duty, Delos 39, 41, 45, 46, 48, 50, 83, 90, 91, 94, 95, 99, 101, 102, 106, 108, 135, 145, 153

East St Louis (IL) 14, 117
Elaine (AR) 13

Index

England 3
Erdington, E.R. 45
Ewing, Don 59, 60–61, 98

Fall, Albert 78, 81
Farmers Security Administration 140
Farrington, Frank 12–13, 30, 31, 54, 57, 69, 70, 80, 92, 103, 146
Finley, Alan 47, 75, 91
Fontenetta, Phillip 54, 57, 94, 104, 105
Foreman, Maj. Gen. Milton J. 71
Frank, Leo 118
Franks, Bobby 137
Frattini, Steve 154

Galigan, George 92
Garvey, Marcus 134
Glen, Otis 105, 110
Gompers, Samuel 11–13, 70, 89
Goodman, William 98, 99
Gotti, John 134, 141
Grace, Bert 60, 93, 94, 98, 101, 103, 104
Graves, Harold 58
Greater Marion Association 24, 45
Green, Ed 75
Green, William 45
Greenhouse, Oscar 92
"Gropher mlnes" 139

Hall, Percy 92, 99
Hamilton, Charles 33, 45
Hammond, John Hays 141
Harding, Warren G. 6, 16–18, 29, 68, 69, 70, 79, 83, 84, 85, 87, 89, 93, 117, 141, 145
Hargraves Detective Agency 33, 36
Harper, Roland 112–113
Harrisburg (IL) 134
Harrison, Fred 58
Harrison, George 58
Hartwell, D.T. 50, 89, 90, 91, 93, 94, 95, 98, 102, 103, 123, 145
Hemingway, Ernest 17
Henderson. Jordy or Gerodie 47, 48, 75, 77, 96
Hepburn, Mitchell 131
Herrin (IL) 19, 24–27, 61, 135, 137, 138, 139, 130, 149
"to herrin" 137
Hertel, Charles 116
Hiller, Peter 57, 93, 94, 100, 101, 103
Hoffman, Clare 130
Hoffman, Howard 59, 60, 96, 97, 98, 102

Holmes, Sherman 36, 57
Homold, Dr. F.C. 69
Hoover, Herbert 40, 78, 85
Hoover, J. Edgar 10
Horsley, Luther 92
Howard, Oscar 55, 93, 99, 102, 104, 106
Howat, Alex 29, 30, 48, 55, 105
Hudgens, Guy Bell 77
Hughes, Charles Evan 84
Hughes, Fox 48, 49, 136
Hunter, Col. Sam 39, 40, 41, 42, 45, 48, 50, 51, 52, 54, 61, 68, 89, 108, 109, 110

Illinois Coal Operators Association 31, 69
Illinois Ordinance Plant 140, 141
Industrial Workers of the World (IWW) 13

Jacobs, Mabelle 76
John Birch Society 123
Johnson City (IL) 25, 133
Jones, Bernard 53, 54, 101

Kamp, Joseph P. 130
Kansas 29
Karas, Chris 38
Keely, Grover 47
Kerr, A.W. 91, 95, 96, 97, 99, 102, 103, 104, 105
Ku Klux Klan 133, 134, 135, 136, 137
Kubinis, Ignace 61, 77

Lattimar Massacre 10
Lawrence, Otis 54
Leopold and Loeb 137
Lester, William J. 28, 32, 33, 34, 35, 38, 41, 42, 43, 44, 45, 48, 50, 68, 73, 95, 96, 104, 107, 108, 109, 125, 126, 128, 130, 136, 142, 143, 145
Lewis, A.C. 98
Lewis, John L. 10–13, 28, 29, 31, 32, 42–43, 69, 78, 89, 98, 119, 120, 121, 129, 144, 146, 147
Lincoln. Abraham 19, 115
Little, Frank 13
Lovestone, Jay 124
Lylton, Arthur J. 126
Lyndon, George E., Jr. 73

Macy, Fred 70, 73
USS Maine 2

168

Index

Malkovich, Antonio 77, 104
Mann, Leva 59, 60, 93, 94, 98, 99, 101, 103
Marion (IL) 24, 87, 141
Matewan (WV) 19, 14, 15
McAdoo, William 17
McDowell, C.K. 33, 37, 38, 41, 42, 44, 45, 46, 47, 48, 49, 50, 53, 54, 55, 56, 75, 76, 96, 99, 100, 102, 104, 115, 129
McGowan, William 73, 77, 98
McIntoff, Charlie 94
McLaren, A.B. 50
Mencken, H.L. 17, 137
Middlekauff, L.W. 90, 103, 104
Miller, Arthur 77
Mitchell, Thomas 96
Moakes Crossing 55, 56, 61, 107
Molly McGuires 9
Moore v. Dempsey 13
Morrison, Sidney 45
Mother Jones 19, 39
Myers, Henry Lee 79, 80

National Association for the Advancement of Colored People (NAACP) 115, 117
Nelson, George 101
Nelson, Toliver 37

Obama, Barrack 149
Officer, Robert 51, 99
Ogle, Alfred 70
O'Rourke, Patrick 37, 59, 60, 61, 72, 99, 106, 107, 145
Overman, Lee Slater 119

Pace, A.T. 24, 71, 93, 136
Palmer, A. Mitchell 12
Pendland, Nathan 94
Pershing, Gen. John "Black Jack" 84
Petkewicz, Joe 48, 77
Polo, Marco 7
Potz, Ignance 72
Powell, Paul 139
Prager, Robert 116
press reaction to the massacre 63–68, 72
Prohibition 133, 134
Pullet, G.H. 118

Renard, Earl 25
Resendiz, Jose 83
Richardson, Al 38
Riddle, Henry 103

Robin Hood 133
Roosevelt, Franklin D. 16, 131, 132
Roosevelt, Ted 131
Rose, Edward 57, 61
Rothstein, Arthur 140
Ryan, George 72

St. Valentine's Day Massacre 138
Scotland 3, 8
Scott, Latin 118
Searles, Ellis 82
Shaffer, Charlie 46
Shafter, John 39, 48, 109
Shields, William 118
Shipman, Dr. O.F. 60, 99
Shoemaker, John 48, 57, 76
Small, Ida 72
Small, Len 43, 68, 71, 72, 88, 104, 108, 110, 139, 144
Sneed, William 35, 48, 72, 108, 129
Soprano, Tony 133
Steam Shovel Men's Union 35, 42, 43
Stimpson, Henry 141
Storm or Strome, S.E. 39, 48, 109

Taft, William Howard 35
USS Texas 2
Thaxton, Melvin 32, 39, 41, 42, 45, 46, 48, 54, 61, 91, 93, 108, 109, 153
Theophrastus 7
Thomas, Ora 135
Tracy, Robert 105
Trovillian, Hal 25, 135
Trumka, Dick 148
Trump, Donald 3, 16, 145
Tulsa (OK) 13
Tuttle, Arthur 69

United Mine Workers of America (UMWA) 9–12, 24, 29, 82, 119, 138, 139, 141
United Mine Workers of America v. Coronado 126
"The Untouchables" 133

Valentino, Rudolph 101

Wales 9
Watkins, Will 107
Webb, Sylvester 94
West City (IL) 136
White, William Allan 85
Williams, Howard 135
Williams, Whitey 58

Index

Williamson County (IL) 19, 23–24, 32, 49, 87, 93, 107, 126, 129, 133, 134, 139, 140, 142, 144, 149, 151
Willis, Hugh 32, 46, 50, 56, 63, 71, 92, 95, 100, 104, 105, 108, 146, 153
Wilson, Vernon 73

Workers Party of America 124
Wyatt, David 116

Yabolanski, Joseph 147
Young, S. Glen 133, 135

www.ingramcontent.com/pod-product-compliance
Ingram Content Group UK Ltd.
Pitfield, Milton Keynes, MK11 3LW, UK
UKHW042016140426
5217IPUK00015B/1202